Longman

LONGMAN GROUP LIMITED
London
*Associated companies, branches and representatives
throughout the world*

© Longman Group 1976

First published 1976
Third impression 1980
ISBN 0 582 20523 9

Filmset by BAS Printers Limited, Wallop, Hampshire.
Printed in Hong Kong by Wing Tai Cheung Printing Co. Ltd.

Contents

Acknowledgements

For assistance in the preparation of notes on the songs we are grateful to Roy Palmer, Birmingham Reference Library, Birmingham Museum and Art Gallery, British Museum, Public Record Office, English Folk Dance and Song Society, Plymouth City Library, Miss Maud Karpeles, Mrs R. V. Williams, A. L. Lloyd, Ewan MacColl and the people who made and sang the songs.

We are grateful to the following for permission to reproduce copyright material:
John Addy for the letter from Colonel de Lancey to the Secretary of State 1792; Miss Fanny F. Andrews for extracts from *The Complete Torrington Diaries* edited by C. Bruyn Andrews 1934–8 reprinted in 1970 (a one-volume edition abridged by Miss F. Andrews was published by Eyre & Spottiswoode (Publishers) Ltd in 1954); Birmingham Reference Library (Local Studies Department) for 'The Tokens' and 'A desperate boxing match'; Brown, Smith & Ferguson, Ltd. for the tune of 'Poor Paddy works on the railway' from W. B. Whall, *Sea Songs and Shanties* 1910; The Syndics of the Cambridge University Library for the words of 'The Collier Lass' from *Madden Collection of Ballads*; Cusworth Hall Museum, Doncaster for an extract from the *J. Goodchild MSS*; Derby Borough Libraries, Wardwick, Derby for extracts from the *Strutt Papers* and an extract from *Derby Mercury 1785* in Derby Local History Library; The County Archivist, Derbyshire Record Office for an extract from 'Notice of Bankruptcy' 1952/E4 and extracts from the *Records of Belper Petty Sessions*; Eyre & Spottiswoode (Publishers) Ltd. for an extract from 'Select Committee on the State of Children employed in Manufactories 1816' from *English Historical Documents* Vol XI edited by A. Aspinall and E. A. Smith and for an extract from 'Report of Commissioners on Employment of Children in Factories 1833' from *English Historical Documents* Vol. XII edited by G. M. Young and W. D. Hancock; Earl Fitzwilliam and his Trustees for extracts from the *Wentworth Woodhouse Muniments* and an extract from *Rockingham Papers*; The Folk Song Society for the tune 'Henry's Downfall' from *Journal of the Folk Song Society*, Vol. II; S. W. Fraser for extracts from the *Spencer Stanhope Muniments*; Hutchinson & Company (Publishers) Ltd. for an extract from *The Farington Diary* 1922 edited by Greig; The Institution of Mechanical Engineers for an extract from 'The Brandling Papers'; P. Burgoyne-Johnson for 'Bill' and two letters from *Charles Brandling Letter Book*; Mrs A. H. Kay for 'A Letter' from *The Harrison Papers*; Lancashire Records Office for an extract from 'Quarter Sessions Orders 1784', 'A Letter from Henry Blundell to Henry Dundas' October 1792, the words of the song 'Come all you cotton weavers' from J. Harland, *Ballads and Songs of Lancashire* 1865 and letters from Miners to Jonathan Blundell November 1843 from *Blundell Colliery MSS*; the author for

'The Coalowner and the pitman's wife' and 'The Cock-fight' from *Come all ye Bold Miners* 1952 by A. L. Lloyd published by Lawrence & Wishart, Ltd; the Editor and Workers' Music Association Ltd. for the words of 'Poor Paddy works on the railway', and for the words and tune of 'The Best Little Doorboy' from *Shuttle and Cage* edited by Ewan MacColl; Manchester Public Libraries for 'Opposition by Spinners to this Bill'; Manchester University Press for an extract from *Iron and Steel in the Industrial Revolution* 1924 (Reprinted 1963) by T. S. Ashton, extracts from *The Strutts and the Arkwrights* by Fitton and Wadworth and 'Contract' from *The Coal Industry of the 18th Century* by T. S. Ashton and J. Sykes; Newcastle-upon-Tyne City Libraries for an extract from *Tomlinson MSS* in the Newcastle-upon-Tyne Local History Library; Northumberland County Record Office for an extract from the *Cully MSS* in the Northumberland Record Office; City of Plymouth Public Libraries for the tune 'A nutting we will go' from *Baring-Gould MSS* LXXXIII; the Keeper of the Public Records for *Inventory of Joseph Walker*; the Agent for the Cecil Sharp Estate for two tunes: 'Three Pretty Maidens' and 'The Bonny Labouring Boy' both from the *Cecil Sharp Collection*; Sheffield City Libraries for extracts from the *Clarke Records*, an article 'Opening of the Sheffield–Rotherham Railway' from *Doncaster, Nottingham and Lincoln Gazette* 30th November 1838, an extract from *Tibbets Collection* TC684, an extract from 'Sheffield Mechanics Library' 15th September 1832 from *Miscellaneous Documents* 485M, an extract from 'Regulations of Mechanics Library' from *Leader Collection* LC513, an extract from *Cuttings relating to Sheffield* Vol. II and an extract from *Cuttings relating to Sheffield* Vol. X; Sheffield Newspapers Ltd. for an advertisement from *Sheffield Telegraph* January 1843 and an article 'Railway excursion' from *Sheffield Telegraph* 30th June 1923.

We regret that we have been unable to trace the copyright holder of the tune used for 'The Collier Lass' and Alan Lomax the collector of 'The best little doorboy', and would appreciate receiving any information that would enable us to do so.

Introduction

Instant interest is desirable in any book, but it is not the only quality a teacher looks for in a book of this kind. One hopes also to find the sort of material to arouse that appreciative interest which grows with a sympathetic understanding of the changes and problems of the Industrial Revolution.

In selecting the material, we have tried to invoke the spirit of the Then and There Series, by aiming at actuality, and we hope that the illustrations and photo-reproductions of some of the documents help to achieve this. We have deliberately concentrated on a somewhat limited number of persons and places rather than trying to ensure that every town and county in Britain gets a mention. We hope that by focusing on a narrower field, pupils will obtain a greater sense of reality, and may more easily discover what a variety of source material is available in every area.

We have had to assume that pupils using this book will either know something of the Industrial Revolution before studying the documents, or that they will be able to go from an extract to a more general account of the points referred to in it. The relevant titles in the Then and There Series may profitably, but not necessarily, be used for this purpose.

We have left the use of the book as open as possible, hoping however that it will not be given to pupils merely to 'work through'. We have included questions on individual documents and groups of documents, as well as suggestions for research in this book and elsewhere. We hope that none of our suggestions will deter teachers from selecting documents and framing questions to suit their own purposes.

JOHN ADDY
E. G. POWER

I
Inventors
and
Factory
Owners

Background and interests

When we start to learn about an inventor or an employer in the Industrial Revolution we generally picture him only in his work—tinkering with machinery, gloating over the month's profit, or striding around being harsh (or, in a few cases, kind) to his workers.

It is easy to forget that employers, especially in the early stages of industrial change, were not in a class separate from their fellow men. They were likely to be small farmers or tradesmen, with a second occupation besides the one for which they are remembered. They had the normal human experiences of growing up, courtship, marriage and raising a family. When they looked back over their lives the highlights were not each additional thousand pounds annual profit, but more likely the finding of a good wife, the turning-out of a son as a gentleman, or the move to a fine new house.

1 Farmer-nailers

Warwick Wed noon Octr 7, King St. Cheapside Thursday Even^g

Dear James

I wrote so far yesterday & was prevented by the arrival of the coach (which conveyed me to Coventry) from proceeding further. I arrived safe in London about nine o'clock last even^g after a cold but comfortable ride & have this day delivered all my acc^{ts} except two & only made one appointment. Several are complaining of quality & I am afraid I shall feel the effects of dearer Iron nails. This is a needless uphill work for scarcity of trade is bad enough without complaints. They complain so of THE POINTS BEING HOLLOW. . . .

Have they finished getting out the potatoes? Has Joseph been paid & did you remember the milk? W^m must sow the Sandbed as early as he can. He may then plough the wheat stubble on the hillside & it may be cleaned for a fallow. Chas. must pull the turnip field enough to supply the cows with tops. He must also be particular in excercising the mare every day & keep her knees well greased. Had you many nails in on Monday? Mour & Co. are complaining of the tale—say they are buying lighter nails out of Staffordshire. They brought forward a bag of large 14lbs. They are having 16lbs from Staffs. As far as I can at present judge am afraid shall not have many orders —everything seems very flat. . . .

Your affec^{te} Brother

Thomas

The Harrison Papers, Mrs. A. H. Kay

Glossary and notes

Before the Factory System came in most workers combined two or more jobs as a family working unit. Father farmed, sons farmed and wove, mother and daughters spun and helped with the poultry and so on. You may not have thought that employers often combined two businesses also. A miller might also be a farmer; a butcher might also be a coal merchant. In this letter Thomas Harrison writes from London to his brother James. The Harrisons were nailmasters of Belper, in Derbyshire.

The letter was written in 1842, but nailing was still carried on under the domestic system at that time.

POINTS BEING HOLLOW   nails with faulty points or ends.

The INVENTORY *of* JOSEPH WALKER, *Nailer, of Stubben House, in the parish of Ecclesfield, 21st December, 1729*

	£	s	d
IMPRIMIS, his purse and apparell	3	0	0
(House). One Range one p^r of Tongues 3 Iron potts		12	0
One Great Table 6 Chairs One Ovall Table One Long Settle One Dresser	1	1	0
All the pewter One Warming Pan		14	0
In the parlour. One Range 2 Chairs One Long Table 2 Chists One Ovell Table One Desk		14	0
One Bed wth Beding & Hangings belonging to it	3	0	0
In the passage. One Bed & Beding One Cupboard	1	0	0
In the Chamber Over the House. 2 Great ARKS One p^r of BEDSTOCKS 1 Chist 6 Sacks	1	4	0
In the Kitching. One Range One pott 1 Tubb 1 FLASKITT 1 Churne 1 KITT		10	0
3 Wheels and all other HUSTLEMENT		6	8
In ye Smithy. 1 p^r of Old Bellows & all other work Tools		10	0
2 Old Carts 1 plow 3 Horses wth Gears belonging to them	18	0	8
3 Cows 2 Heifers 2 Calves One Swine	14	5	0
In the Barn, Hay and Corn & for Corn Sown & plowing in the Land	20	10	0
One Hay Stack in the field	2	10	0
	67	6	8
	(67	17	4)

John Hive, Robert Mathewman, Henry Waterhouse

The Borthwick Institute of Historical Research, York

Glossary and notes

INVENTORY   detailed accounts of moveable goods and chattels left by people, listed after their death. Their belongings are valued item by item for the purpose of sharing them out.

JOSEPH WALKER   the father of Samuel Walker who later founded the famous ironworks at Rotherham.

IMPRIMIS   the first (item).

ARKS   chests for meal or flour.

BEDSTOCKS   the framework of a wooden bed.

FLASKITT   a flask.

KITT   a small barrel.

HUSTLEMENT   old junk.

When I was quite a child my father removed from Hall i' th' Wood to Oldham, and there two brothers and a sister were born. I recollect that soon after I was able to walk I was employed in the cotton manufacture. My mother used TO BAT the COTTON WOOL on a

3

wire RIDDLE. It was then put into a deep brown MUG with a strong LEY of soap suds. My mother then tucked up my petticoats about my waist, and put me in the tub to tread upon the cotton at the bottom. When a second riddleful was batted I was lifted out and I was placed in the mug, and I again trode it down. This process was continued until the mug became so full that I could no longer safely stand in it, when a chair was placed beside it, and I held on by the back. When the mug was quite full, the soap suds were poured off, and each separate dollop of wool well squeezed to free it from moisture. They were then placed on the bread-rack under the beams of the kitchen-loft to dry.

Gilbert French, 'The Life of Samuel Crompton', 1860

Glossary and notes

SAMUEL GEORGE CROMPTON   born in 1781, the son of Samuel Crompton who invented the Mule. Here he describes how his parents employed him in the domestic system of cotton manufacture.

TO BAT   to clean.

COTTON WOOL   raw cotton.

RIDDLE   coarse type of sieve.

MUG   earthenware tub.

LEY   covering.

4 Jedediah proposes to Elizabeth Wollatt

Blackwell Feb. 3 : 1755

Dear Betty,

Since our first acquaintance, which is now many years ago, I have often wrote to you, but never in a strain like this; nor did I ever think I shoud; for tho' we was more intimately acquainted than since and tho' I then thought you had some degree of KINDNESS for me, yet as my conduct and behaviour to you has been such as cou'd neither raise nor continue your regard, together with the years that has passed since then, (for time often puts a PERIOD to Love as well as all other events) I did not think you coud remember me with the least pleasure or satisfaction, but rather the contrary; but whaen I was at London and had the opportunity of seeing you something or other told me (tho' perhaps nothing more than the last glance of your eye when I bad you farewell) that you looked on me with an Eye of tenderness, nay one is so apt to speak as they wish, I had liked to have said Love; and if so, that one generous instance of truth and constancy has made a greater and more lasting impression on my mind, than all the united charms of Beauty, Wit and fortune of your sex, so far as I have had opportunity of conversing were ever able to make: therefore it is upon this foundation I presume to tell you, that from a wandering, inconstant, roving swain I am become intirely yours: I am ready to be all you cou'd wish me to be, if you Lov'd me, and which is all I wish, your Husband. . . .

And now, if ever you had any kindness for me, if ever I did or said anything to give you either delight or pleasure, let it not be in vain that I now ask, nor torture me with silence and suspense; by so doing you will lay the highest obligation on one who is in every sence of the word is your sincere Lover.

J: Strutt

Derby Central Library, Strutt Collection

Glossary and notes

Jedediah Strutt was a small farmer at the time he wrote this letter, in 1755. Elizabeth Wollatt, like many young women of the rather better-off working class, was in service, that is she was a servant to a richer family. Perhaps you will think that Jedediah takes a long time to get to the point. The dots represent as much again of the same sort of stuff.

About a fortnight later Betty wrote back to say yes. They were married and three years later Jedediah had invented his Derby Rib machine for stocking knitting and was having it patented. They tried to borrow money from Betty's former employer to meet the expenses (see extract 23, p. 26).

KINDNESS affection.

PERIOD end.

5 Getting on in the world

a Derby July 2nd 1775
My Dear & Honour'd Father,
I received your letter yesterday & was glad to hear you got well to London. . . .

Bro: Wm. & George set off this morning, about 11 o'clock they will stay at Cromford all night & go to Chesterfield tomorrow George says he will be very good & Joe has been good today they both send their duty to you & joe desires you will bring his Cousin joe down with you if he gets better.

Mr Arkwright came here on wednesday night & brought his daughter a very pretty letter from her Brother &—would you think it —a very elegant little watch which he bought for her at Manchester on Thursday morning they set off from here to Birmingham, my sister and Miss Arkwright in genteel riding dresses & provided with pen & Ink & Memorandum Books that they may see which writes the best journal. . . .

I have made you a night shirt & shall send it tomorrow in the bag along with the shirt that you left to have a button hole made in the wrist band when you receive that you will have 7 shirts 6 STOCKS & three pocket handkerchiefs.

It is almost dark: so I wish you a very good night,
& am with the greatest affection
your dutiful Daughter
E. Strutt

Tuesday
My Aunt Woollatt desires to be remembered to you & will be obliged to you to buy for her a handsome silver Cream Jug such a one as you would buy for yourself.

b Derby July 24 1775
My Dear Father,
. . . FINDERN is a strange desolate place now — I used to think it very fine & have spent many a happy day there, but I think I am happier now—everybody is surprised when they consider what we are, and what we have been. I often think of it & I never think of it but my heart & eyes o'erflow with joy & gratitude. I can never thank you enough, nor ever repay the vast, vast debt I owe you. . . .

[Elizabeth Strutt]

Derby Central Library, Strutt Collection

Glossary and notes

These two letters were written twenty years later. They are from Elizabeth, Jedediah's daughter. William, George and Joseph were her brothers. Mr Arkwright is, of course, Richard Arkwright the inventor of the water frame, and Jedediah's partner in business. The two families were on very friendly terms. Notice that Jedediah still has some of his clothes made at home, as was usual among the class of small farmers, tradesmen and craftsmen.

In the second letter Elizabeth refers directly to the way in which the family has risen in the world.

STOCKS   kind of cravat.

FINDERN   the village where her mother's home was.

6 A schoolboy's letter, from Jedediah's son

Dear Pappa   July 27 Chesterfield 1770

I Received yours a few days since & was greatly rejoiced to hear from you. I like school full as well as I expected, & will improve as much as ever I can, both in manners, & learning: for M^r. Astley takes a great deal of pains. I received a letter from home last saturday, they were all very well. Did Brother wright to you about some books which I were to have because you was saying you could get them at London. If he has not I should be glad the next time you wright you would mention it to him; because M^r. Astley gave him an account of what sorts I must have; for I shall want them as soon as possible. I have begun of making themes, & like it very well, & I hope shall continue so, &

intend to have a good many against I come home,
which I expect to do at christmas: but Mr Astley
gives no holidays, but leaves it to their friends.
But they all go & for that reason it will be very
disagreeable to stay by myself. But you will
tell me when you come hither which I hope will be soon & bring
cousin joe with you to Derby. I often think of
your kind letter which you sent me but you never
told me how you did, for I made shift to read it.
Mr Astley wishes I might learn to wright & I do to
because if I do not it will be too late; for I should chuse to
wright better than what I do. Miss Malkin whent to
Derby last week, & is not come back yet, but intends
coming in a few days. I saw miss Nanny last week, she
was very well. I shall wright home soon, because I never
have since I came; & Sister thinks me long, for I pro-
mised her I would wright home very often but I have
had nothing to say. I am very glad Sister likes London,
but Sister told me you will stay a month longer,
but I hope you will not exceed that; I expected Miss Astbury it
would have stayed till you came; for you might have come
togeather. You will give my love to Sister, Uncle, Aunt &
Cousins, & all that inquire after me.

I am your most dutifull
& affectionate Son.
George Strutt.

This letter to Jedediah is from George, who, according to the previous letter was setting off for Chesterfield on July 2nd. You will see now that his older brother William was taking him to boarding school there. Now that the Strutts were becoming wealthier it was important that the boys should receive a good education, not just to make them able to help manage the business, but to make them able to behave like and mix with 'gentlemen of quality'. Notice that he is asking his father to buy him his school books in London.

7 A school bill

Derby Central Library, Local History Collection

This is a bill from the sort of school which George was at. Notice the expenses and 'extras'. Notice also when the school re-opens. As George Strutt's letter says, there were often no regular terms and holidays.

8 Richard Arkwright's grand house

June 14th 1789
Below Matlock a new creation of SR. RD. ARKWRIGHT's is started up, which has crowded the village of Cromford with cottages, supported by his three magnificent cotton mills. There is so much water, so much rock, so much population, and so much wood, that it looks like a Chinese town. At our inn (the Black Dog) T. Bush having gone forward, had prepared, (as he knows well to do) our beds, and our stables. We took a meand'ring walk around these little mills, bridges and cascades; and went to where Sr. R. Arkwright is building for himself a grand house (WENSLEY CASTLE) in the same CASTELLATED stile as one sees at Clapham; and *really* he has made a *happy* choice of ground, for by sticking it up on an unsafe bank, he contrives to overlook, not see, the beauties of the river, and the surrounding scenery. It is the house of an overseer surveying the works, not of a gentleman wishing for retirement and quiet. But light come, light go, Sr. Rd. has honourably made his great fortune; and so let him still live in a great cotton mill!

June 19th 1790
After a grand dressing . . . and a long breakfast, I took a short walk to look at the weather, and at Sr. Rd. Arkwright's new house. The inside is now finishing; and it is really, within, and without, an effort of inconvenient ill taste; built so high as to overlook every beauty, and to catch every wind; the approach is dangerous; the ceilings are of GEW-GAW fret work; the small circular stair-case, like some in the new-built houses of Marybone, is so dark and narrow, that people cannot pass each other; I asked a workman if there was a library? Yes, answer'd he, at the foot of the stairs. Its dimensions are 15 feet square; (a small counting house;) and having the perpendicular lime stone rock within 4 yards, it is too dark to read or write in without a candle ! There is likewise a music room; this is upstairs, is 18 feet square, and will have a large organ in it; what a scheme! What confinement! At Clapham they can produce nothing equal to this, where ground is sold by the yard.

Andrews, ed. 'The Torrington Diaries', 1954

Glossary and notes

In 1789 and again in 1790 Lord Torrington, a member of an old noble family, was touring in the area and made these entries in his diary.

SR. RD. ARKWRIGHT began life as a barber, and became probably more famous than any other inventor or factory owner. Like many other self-made men he knew that he was not very well educated and he tried, late in life, to improve his spelling and English expression by spending two hours a day in study. His spelling certainly needed some improvement (see extract 10 p. 13). He was given a knighthood in 1786, and in 1788 he began building a grand mansion for himself at Cromford, so that he could live in a manner suitable to a real gentleman.

WENSLEY CASTLE   the correct name of the house is Willersley Castle.

CASTELLATED   looking like castle battlements.

GEW-GAW   over decorated.

2
Inventions

Introduction

Almost all inventions were made to remedy some drawback in an existing industrial process—a drawback which everyone in the particular business was aware of. Because of this, it was not unusual for two or more men to invent a similar method or new device about the same time. Invention was a continuing process, with many modifications and improvements being made to the first machines by other people in later years. Most inventions came into use fairly slowly. Employers and workers were reluctant to try them, until they were convinced that they would work. People generally were very cautious about 'progress' in the eighteenth century.

In the mines the use of naked candles had frequently caused serious explosions so it was desirable that someone should design a new kind of lamp that could be used in safety. George Stephenson in Northumberland, Ben Biram at Elsecar and Sir Humphry Davy all designed lamps that could be used. In the end the Davy Lamp became the standard model.

When charcoal for smelting iron began to be difficult to obtain due to the wholesale cutting of woods, Abraham Darby attempted to find a new way of smelting by using coal. He found that raw coal was no use but when turned into coke then it could replace charcoal. Likewise it was necessary to find a quicker way to produce steel than the slow Huntsman process. Sir Henry Bessemer experimented with a method of removing impurities from iron by blowing air through molten iron. The process, when successful, reduced the price of steel and speeded up the process from days to hours.

The flying shuttle, the jenny, the water frame, the mule and the power loom are the best known of the textile inventions. They were all improved on, after the first type, sometimes by the inventor himself, sometimes by one of the workmen who used the machine. There were also many new devices which simplified the work of preparing the cotton and wool for spinning, making the yarn ready for weaving, and finishing the woven or knitted material before it was sold.

Some people opposed these inventions on the grounds that they would take away their livelihood and thought that the old domestic system ought to be preserved. Petitions were sent to Justices of Peace to have the inventions suppressed but since they saw the advantages that these would bring in increasing trade they gave their wholehearted support to them.

In the textile industry

9 The Helmshore Jenny

Helmshore Local History Society. C. Aspin and S. D. Chapman, 'James Hargreaves and the Spinning Jenny', 1964

Glossary and notes

The Spinning Jenny in the picture is one made recently by members of the local History Society in Helmshore, Lancashire. Only the materials which were available in Hargreaves's time were used to build it, and it really does spin cotton.

You may find it stated in some books that Hargreaves named his spinning machine after his wife Jenny. In fact, her name was Elizabeth. Gin, ginny or jenny were terms commonly used for any piece of machinery in the eighteenth century.

10 Problems at Cromford

Cromford Marh 2d 72

Sir,

Yours yisterday came to hand together with a bill from Mr. Need value 60lb. I have sent a little cotton spun on the one spindle & find no Difficanty in Geting it from the Bobbin & Dubeld & Twistd in the maner you see it at one opration. One hand I think will do 40 or 50lb. of it in one day from the bobins it is spun upon, that is in the new whay.

A yonge man was hear this wheek sade he had spoke to you: this is his Riteing I send Inclosed. What do you think of him, he seems a Likely person but has all to lern. I am afraide no one man will know all that I shold Expect he might.

I asked Mr. Whard to get some Led pipes to bring the (water) into the mill; they are conuinially fetching. It might be Brought in the Rooms. Wold it not be best to fix a Crank to one of the lying shafts to work a pump or Ingon in case of fire. Bring the belts with you. Desire ward to send those other Locks and allso Some sorts of Hangins for the sashes he and you may think best and some good Latches & Catches for the out doors and a few for the inner ons allso and a Large Knoker or a Bell to First door. I am Determind for the feuter to Let no persons in to Look at the wor[k]s except spining. The man Mr. Whard Bot. the ash Board from calld for his money & says he will send the other shortly. I am tired with riteing so Long a Letter & think you can scairsley Reed it. Excuse haist

and am yours' &c
R. Arkwright

Quoted in Seymour Jones, 'The Invention of Roller Drawing in Cotton Spinning'

Glossary and notes

This letter was written by Richard Arkwright to Jedediah Strutt in the early days of the revolution in textiles, when the water frame was in the experimental stage. Arkwright was trying out his invention, putting the finishing touches to his mill, and looking for bright young men to train as mechanics. Notice his bad spelling and grammar.

11 The dressing frame and steam loom

Before the invention of the DRESSING FRAME, one weaver was required to each steam loom, at present a boy or girl, 14 or 15 years of age, can manage two steam looms, and with their help can weave three and a half times as much as the best hand weaver. The best hand weavers seldom produce a piece of uniform evenness; indeed it is next to impossible for them to do so, because a weaker or stronger blow with the LATHE immediately alters the thickness of the cloth and after an interruption of some hours, the most experienced weaver finds it difficult to recommence with a blow of precisely the same force as the one with which he left off. In steam looms, the lathe gives a steady, certain blow, and when once regulated by the engineer, moves with the greatest precision from the beginning to the end of the piece. Cloth made by these looms, when seen by those manufacturers who employ hand weavers, at once excites admiration and a consciousness that their own workmen cannot equal it.

Richard Guest, 'Compendious History of the Cotton Manufacture', 1823

Glossary and notes

DRESSING FRAME   a minor invention, made in 1803 by Thomas Johnson of Bradbury in Cheshire. Dressing meant stiffening the warp threads by coating them with size (a kind of weak glue). Using the dressing frame this could be done all at once, before the loom was set going. The loom needed no more attention then until the whole length of cloth had been woven.

LATHE   the part of the loom which beat the weft into the warp.

1st. Resolved that it is the Unanimous Opinion of this Court, that the sole Cause of the Riots, Tumults and Insurrections, that have lately happened in the County of Lancaster is owing to the Erection of certain Mills and Engines within the said County, for the Manufacturing of Cotton, which in the Idea of the Persons Assembled tend to Depreciate the price of Labour.

2d. Resolved Unanimously, that it is the Opinion of this Court, after the Examination of many Witnesses, that the Invention and Introduction of the Machines for Carding, Roving, Spinning and Finishing Cotton, has been of the greatest Utility to this Country by the extension and improvement of the Cotton Manufactures and the affording Labour and Subsistance to the Industrious poor, who have not had any pretence for Committing the late Riots from the want of Work.

3d. Resolved that it is the Unanimous Opinion of this Court, that it is impossible, to Restrain the force of Ingenuity, when employed in the Improvement of Manufactures. That any Machines that may have been found, to effectuate that purpose, become the property of the World. That the Destroying them in one Country, only serves to establish them in another, and that if the Legislature was to prevent the Exercise of them in this Kingdom, it would tend to Establish them in Foreign Countrys, which would be highly Detrimental to the Trade of this Country.

Lancashire Record Office, Quarter Sessions Orders, 1780

In 1777 Arkwright leased a group of buildings, including a corn mill and forges, at Birkacre, near Chorley, Lancashire. He established a cotton-spinning factory there, but it was bitterly resented by the local hand- and jenny-spinners. In 1779 it was attacked, along with nine mills belonging to other manufacturers, and the Lancashire J.P.s had to call on the army to suppress the rioters. Meeting in the Court of Quarter Sessions, they later recorded their opinions on the value of the new machines, which had been the cause of all the trouble.

13a An American
spinning frame

b An American
carding machine

Derby Central Library

Glossary and notes

The story of these two illustrations takes us to America. Samuel Slater worked for Jedediah Strutt for several years, and noted carefully how all the machines worked. He then left Belper secretly, and went to the United States, where he set up his own cotton mill. These are two of the machines he built, which began the textile industry in the USA. The spinning frame is a copy of the Arkwright Water Frame. Notice the row of spindles along the front.

The carding machine was used to brush out the tangled raw cotton into a smooth layer of fibres. Carding was originally done by putting the cotton on a board set thick with small wire teeth and brushing it with another toothed block held in the hand.

In this machine, raw cotton spread out in a mat is fed in at the right hand side of the picture. It is held by the teeth on the revolving drum and the fibres are 'combed' by the teeth set in the covering over the top. (This is in sections, some of which have been lifted off.) At the left hand side, the carded cotton is eased off the drum by a metal plate. It was then fed through a funnel and came out as a very loose 'rope' of cotton. The funnel is not shown in this picture.

14 A stocking frame

Nottingham Public Libraries. Local History Library

The stocking-frame was a vital machine in the textile industry of the Midlands. This picture shows the basic type of frame on which yarn was knitted up into stockings or other garments. The knitter sat on the narrow bench seat. Notice the bolt fixing in the slots cut in the upright posts. A variety of gadgets to be fitted on to the machine were invented in the late eighteenth century, beginning with the Derby rib device of Jedediah Strutt. All these were to enable the knitter to produce fancy patterns, by varying the number of possible stitches. In the early nineteenth century an amazing variety of lace-making machines were also invented, all based on the old stocking-frame. (See p. 106).

15 Defending a patent

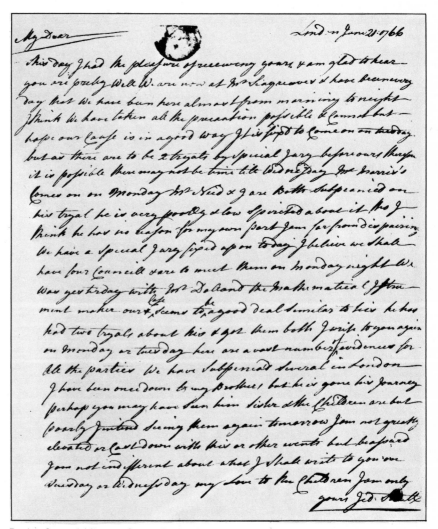

Derby Central Library, Strutt Collection

It will help you to read this if you know the letter 's' was sometimes written to look like the letter 'f'. This was always done in a word containing a 'ss' or where the letter 's' preceded a vowel.

To get a patent, an inventor had to prove that the main ideas for the machine were his own, and not copied nor stolen from someone else, and that it really was a new invention, and not just a slightly altered version of something which was already in use. When the government Patent Office granted patent rights to an inventor, he alone could legally build and use that particular machine for fourteen years. He could, however, allow other people to use it if he wished. In that case the other users had to pay the owner of the patent for permission. In effect, the law backed him up if he said: 'This is my invention, but you may copy it and use it if you pay me so much money.'

Often trade rivals would try to prove that the inventor was not entitled to a patent, saying, for example, that it was not a really new idea. Then a trial was held, and if his rivals won the case, the inventor's patent rights were cancelled. In this letter Jedediah Strutt is writing to his wife from London. The trial is about his patent for the gadget to do ribbed knitting on a stocking-frame. Mr Seagreave was his lawyer. Mr Need was Strutt's partner. Mr Morris was another inventor, from Nottingham.

SUBPOENAED   called as a witness.

Dear Tom,

. . . Mr Gardom has wrote your Brother that Mr Arkwright peremptorily insists upon payment of the £1000 which became due the 1st of last Month & will probably soon endeavour to enforce it—it's wish'd you retain Mr Balguy if he is not already retained for Mr Arkwright & in that case you'll ask him what would be advisable in case Mr A. proceeds by DISTRESS—the putting an intire stop to the machines would be attended with great inconvenience & loss.

Derby Central Library, Pares Collection

16 Avoiding payment

Glossary and notes

Trade rivals were often very jealous of an inventor's success, and might try to avoid paying the amount due to him for permission to use his invention. This letter was written on 25 April 1782 by Thomas Pares Senior to Thomas Pares Junior, who was a solicitor in London, and whose brother was a partner in the firm of Gardom, Pares & Co. This firm had a mill at Calver, near Bakewell. See Textile Business, p. 36.

DISTRESS   here means getting legal authority to seize goods belonging to the firm if they do not pay up.

Friday, Nov. 29, 1782.

THE following incendiary Letter was this Day received by Mr. *Richard Arkwright* :

(C O P Y.)

Mr. Arkwright, at Mr. Brocklehurst's, Manchester.

Sir,   Man. 28th Nov. 1782.

I am very forry to hear that you ftill do all you can to diftrefs the trade of Manr: after you had loft the Caufe in London this town thought you would then have been eafy the remainder of your Time in the patent out. but you ftill keep doing all you can and not only that but you have been heard to fay that you was determin'd to ruin every pœfon that enter'd into that Bufinefs, the purport of this is to advife you that if you d'not withdraw all your profecutions before Dec. is out I am determin'd to lay in wait for you either in this town Nottingham or wherever I moft likely to find you. I will afhure fhute you as your name is what it is dam you do you think the town muft be ruled by fuch a Barber as you. take notice if you are in town on Saturday next I will make an end of you meet you wherever I can. I am not yours, but a friend to the town of Manchefter.

Now I do hereby promife a Reward of ONE HUNDRED GUINEAS to any Perfon or Perfons who fhall difcover or give Information of the Author or Writer of the faid Letter, fo that he os fhe may be profecuted thereon.

RICH. ARKWRIGHT.

N. B. The above Letter was put into the *Manchefter* Office, on *Thurfday* Evening the 28th *November* 1782, after the fix o'Clock Poft was fent off.—Now if the Perfon who put it into the Office will give proper and fufficient Proof who he received it from, he fhall for fuch Information receive Fifty Guineas Reward, by applying to me

RICHARD ARKWRIGHT.

17 A threatening letter

Manchester Central Library, 'Manchester Mercury', 31 December 1782

Glossary and notes

Arkwright had two patents. The first was for the water-frame (1769–1783). The second was for a carding machine (1775–1789). Other cotton manufacturers objected to the second patent and it was cancelled in 1781

Arkwright was furious with those mill-owners and in revenge tried to have the first patent extended to 1789. This in turn made the mill-owners angry with Arkwright. You can see by this letter how unpopular he was, especially in the cotton-spinning town of Manchester. It was printed for everyone to read in the *Manchester Mercury*.

In fact, after much more argument, all Arkwright's claims to patents were cancelled in 1785. It did not matter so much to him, because he was already making thousands of pounds, not out of his patents, but as a factory owner himself.

In the coal and iron industries

I John Moody, do hereby certify whom it may concern that on the 21st of October (1815) at 6 o'clock that evening, I accompany'd Mr. Stephenson and Mr. Wood down the A pit at Killingworth Colliery in purpose to try Mr. Stephenson's first safety lamp at a Blower. But when we came near the Blower it was making more gas than usual that I told Mr. Stephenson and Mr. Wood that if the lamp should deceive him we should be severely burned, but Mr. Stephenson would insist upon the tryal which was very much against my desire. So Mr. Wood and I went out of the way at a distance and left Mr. Stephenson to himself, but we soon heard that the lamp had answer'd his expectations with safety Since that time I have been many times with Mr. Stephenson and Mr. Wood trying his different lamps. I likewise recollect Mr. Stephenson trying many experiments at Blowers before we had any lamp. . . .

Institute of Mechanical Engineers, Brandling Papers

18 The introduction of safety lamps

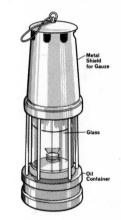

Glossary and notes

The development of the coal and iron industry raised a number of problems that had to be solved. The most serious was the prevention of explosions which so often took place because the miners used candles. In addition to the lamp designed by Sir Humphry Davy, George Stephenson also designed a safety lamp and another lamp was developed by Joshua Biram at Elsecar Colliery. This is an eyewitness account of the testing of George Stephenson's lamp.

Do you think that the particular accidents by explosions which you have . . . described have been much lessened by the introduction of Sir Humphry Davy's safety lamp?

They have, I conceive; but taking the average of 34 years up to the present period, scarcely one half of which we have had the benefit of

19 John Buddle gives evidence about safety lamps

this lamp, the loss of life has been nearly about the same; but I attribute this cause, that we are working mines, from having the advantage of the safety lamp, which we could not possibly have worked without it, and of course they are in a more dangerous situation, and the risk is increased in a very great degree. If we had not the Davy Lamp these mines could not now have been in existence at all; for the only substitute we had, and that was not a safe one, was what we called a steel mill, which was the only means of introducing light, except by the naked flame. . . .

We are entirely within the power of the workmen; and scarcely a month occurs without the punishment of some of them for the mis-management of the Davy lamps; they have been fined, and the magistrates have sent them to the House of Correction for a month yet they will screw off the top of the Davy lamp and expose the naked flame—because they get more light.

Paliamentary Papers, State of the Coal Trade 1829 pp. 32–4

Glossary and notes

In 1829 an enquiry was held into the state of the coal trade and someone questioned the value of Davy's safety lamp in reducing the risk of explosions. John Buddle who gave the evidence knew the reasons why explosions still occurred even when the safety lamp was used.

20 Biram's safety lamp

a . . . this is a common lamp with the wick in the middle and a reflection placed at the back of it; . . . I put it into the inside of a case; in the back of the case is a small contrivance . . . for regulating the wick of the lamp: there is a door in front which admits no air, except through the wire gauze at the bottom; as soon as this lamp is put into an explosive atmosphere, the inflammable gas ignites and burns within the wire gauze; the consequence is no further accession of oxygen can get into the body of the lamp, and the wick, unless the lamp is withdrawn, goes out. . . .

Parliamentary Papers—Report of the Select Committee of the House of Lords, 2 July 1849

Glossary and notes

An enquiry, before a select committee of the House of Lords in July 1849, into the conditions of safety in mines recorded the evidence of Ben Biram of Elsecar who explained the advantages of his safety lamp.

b . . . the Biram miner's lamp emits light fully equal to a naked candle or fourfold that of the Davy Lamp and at a cost in oil of less than one half that of candles.

'Mining Journal' 21 December 1850

Glossary and notes

A comment from the Mining Journal of 1850 states how economical his lamp was in the consumption of oil.

... It was my Husband's Father, whose name he bore [Abraham Darby] who was the first that set on foot the Brass Works at or near Bristol that attempted to mould and cast Iron pots etc., in sand instead of Loam ... in which he succeeded. This first attempt was tryed at an Air Furnace in Bristol. About the year 1709 he came to Shropshire, to Coalbrookdale, and with other partners took a lease of the works which consisted of an old Blast Furnace and some Forges. He here cast Iron Goods in sand out of the Blast Furnace that BLOW'D with wood charcoal; ... Sometime after he suggested the thought that it might be practicable to smelt the Iron from the ore in the Blast Furnace with Pit Coal; Upon this he try'd with raw coal as it came out of the Mines, but it did not answer. He ... had the Coal coak'd into Cynder as is done for drying Malt and then it succeeded to his satisfaction. But he found only one sort of Pit Coal would best suit ... He then erected another Blast Furnace and enlarged the works.

T. S. Ashton, 'Iron and Steel in the Industrial Revolution' 1924, p. 250

Glossary and notes

In 1755 Abiah Darby wrote this letter in which she recorded an account of her father-in-law Abraham Darby and his discovery of how to smelt iron ore by using coke instead of charcoal. This led to a greater and cheaper production of iron which was in demand for armaments, textile machines and steam engines.

BLOW'D   blown with a blast of air.

21 A new discovery in the smelting of iron

King's Topographical Collection, Map Room, British Museum

22 The Bessemer process: its inventor watches and waits for the results

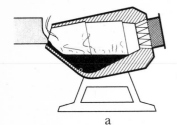

a

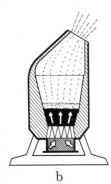

b

c

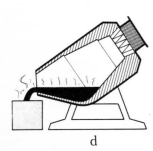

d

I well remember how anxiously I awaited the blowing of the first 7-cwt charge of pig iron. . . . The first element to be attacked by the atmospheric oxygen is the silicon, generally present in pig iron to the extent of 1½ to 2 per cent; it is the white metallic substance of which flint is the acid silicate. Its combustion furnishes a great deal of heat; but it is undemonstrative, a few sparks and hot gases only indicating the fact that something is going quietly on. But after an interval of ten or twelve minutes, when the carbon contained in grey pig iron to the extent of about 3 per cent is seized on by the oxygen, a voluminous white flame is produced, which rushes out of the openings provided for its escape from the upper chamber, and brilliantly illuminates the whole space around. This chamber proved a perfect cure for the rush of slags and metal from the upper central opening of the first converter. I watched with some anxiety for the expected cessation of the flame as the carbon gradually burnt out. It took place almost suddenly, and thus indicated the entire decarburisation of the metal. The furnace was then tapped, when out rushed a limpid stream of INCANDESCENT MALLEABLE iron, almost too brilliant for the eye to rest upon; it was allowed to flow vertically into the . . . ingot mould.

Sir Henry Bessemer, 'An Autobiography', London 1905 pp. 152–3.

Glossary and notes

By the middle of the nineteenth century it was essential to find a new, cheap and quick way of producing steel on a large scale. In 1856 Henry Bessemer was successful and in this letter you can note his anxiety as he watched the process and waited for the results.

INCANDESCENT   brilliant.

MALLEABLE   metal that can be worked without breaking.

Ronan Picture Library

24

3
The
Textile
Business

Introduction

In the eighteenth century, cotton material was passing from the stage of being a luxury to being a necessity. There was a tremendous increase in the demand for this new cloth, which was lighter and more washable than the old woollens, but cheaper than silk. In supplying the demand for Britain, and from overseas as well, the cotton industry was transformed. The employers had to find capital, and workers; harness rivers to drive the machines; master the new spinning processes; and build huge new factories to house the machines and the workers. The factory system, which began in cotton, spread to other textiles, and within a hundred years had become the standard system of industrial production.

Finances

23 Borrowing money

London 3 May
6 o'Clock morning

My Dear
I rec'd your most obligeing Letter yesterday with yt true pleasure, which Love & Gratitude can only feel, & rejoice greatly to hear boath you & my dear little Billy are so well. . . .

I will write again on Satturday next to be at Mansfield on Monday or Tuesday·perhaps you may get somebody to call for it—ye Dr. is pritty well again & I have acquainted him with our scheam which, as far as he understands it thinks it may do very well & he will do all he can for us, & would willingly supply us with ye money. Mr William Cook at ye same time wanted to Borrow of him one thousand pound in order to furnish boath of us he went to ye Bank to sell out but ye War makes ye Stocks run so very low yt he will loose a Hundred pound if he sells out now, & thay will rise as much in proportion if there comes a peace so yt he woud chuse to Borrow for his own use than loose so much money. Ys is a great Disopointmt to me & yet I cannot desire him to act otherwise. . . .

Derby Central Library, Strutt Collection

Glossary and notes

Few of the first inventors and mill-owners had much money to start with. They had to borrow money, or form a partnership. Then they had to build a mill, or convert an old cornmill, or some other building. They had to make arrangements for a waterwheel, or whatever form of power was to be used. They had to build the machinery, or in later times they might buy it second-hand. They had to hire mechanics to take care of the machinery, and other men to be in charge of the workers.

This letter is to Jedediah Strutt from his wife, Elizabeth. In 1758 she went to London to see if they could borrow money from Dr Taylor, a minister for whom she had worked before she was married. They needed the money to go ahead with the development and patenting of the Derby rib device.

If the partners had enough money to stand losses for the first few years they might eventually begin to make a profit. These are the yearly accounts of a firm of five partners who had a mill at Pleasley, near Mansfield in Nottinghamshire. They started in 1785, each putting enough money into the company fund to give a total of £4,200. The first account shows the balance of credits and debits after one year. Compare the three carefully. Notice the *Loss sustained* in the first two. The partners did not draw out any profits for themselves until 1796. They could afford to do this as they all had other businesses. Any profit made was left with the company, so the original capital of £4,200 was up to £14,000 by 1795. (*Cash advanced entry.*)

TWIST   spun cotton or yarn.

COTTON WOOL   raw cotton.

PENSTOCK   trough.

Equipping Mills

26 Advertising for workers

'The Derby Mercury', 16 June 1785 and 15 May 1794

Glossary and notes

The weekly papers often had advertisements like those shown here from the *Derby Mercury*. Advertisements were usually for skilled workmen, clerks, overlookers and mechanics. Ordinary mill hands came from the district around the mill and simply went along there and asked for a job.

WATER WHEELS

DRIVEN SHAFT TO MACHINERY

SPUR GEARS

FLOAT BOARDS

MILL STREAM

UNDERSHOT

TAIL RACE

Used where there is a large volume of slow-moving water. It transmits only about 25% of the power available, which is applied at the bottom of the wheel.

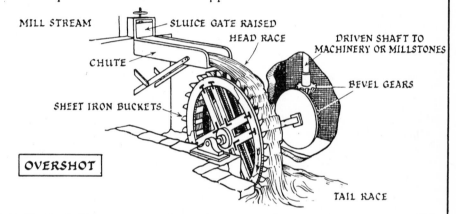

MILL STREAM

SLUICE GATE RAISED

HEAD RACE

DRIVEN SHAFT TO MACHINERY OR MILLSTONES

CHUTE

BEVEL GEARS

SHEET IRON BUCKETS

OVERSHOT

TAIL RACE

Suitable for hilly country with swift streams. It is said to transmit 55% of the available power. The water should hit the wheel at a tangent.

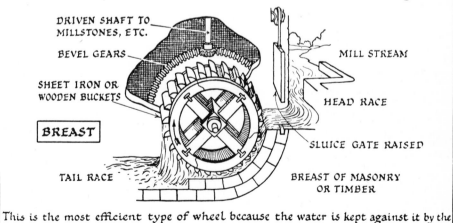

DRIVEN SHAFT TO MILLSTONES, ETC.

BEVEL GEARS

SHEET IRON OR WOODEN BUCKETS

BREAST

MILL STREAM

HEAD RACE

SLUICE GATE RAISED

TAIL RACE

BREAST OF MASONRY OR TIMBER

This is the most efficient type of wheel because the water is kept against it by the breast. It is said to transmit 80% of the power. The water strikes the wheel at axle level.

1. Tenen, 'This England', Part III 1714–1940, Macmillan 1958, p. 123

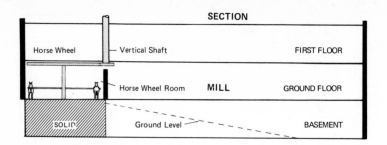

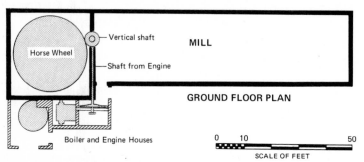

Birmingham Reference Library, David Smith, 'Industrial Archaeology of the East Midlands', Fig. 11. Based on original in Boulton and Watt Collection

Glossary and notes

Almost all the early mills were worked by water power, but some of the very earliest literally used horse power. Arkwright's first spinning frames were driven by a horse-capstan. As the Nottingham mill was not on a river, this method was used there until steam power was available. These drawings are based on sketches made in 1790, when Boulton and Watt were asked to put in a steam engine. Notice how the engine was coupled to the vertical shaft which drove the machines, so that few building alterations were needed.

29 A waterwheel sale

> TO PERSONS CONCERNED IN
> WATER WORKS,
> TO BE SOLD,
> At Ilkiston Cotton Mill, in the county of Derby;
> A WATER WHEEL, close Buckets, suitable for
> either breast or overfall, 20 feet diameter, 6
> wide; together with an excellent Shaft, and Spen
> Wheel, 16 feet diameter, with Cast Iron Segments;
> the whole in good condition, being nearly new.
> Also, 6 Cast Iron Pipes, and 2 Working Barrels,
> 23 inches diameter, the Pipes 9, and the Working
> Barrels 10 feet long.
> Ilkiston Cotton Mill is 9 miles from Derby, and 8
> from Nottingham, close to the Erewash Canal, which
> joins the Cromford and Trent Navigations; the whole
> is now at work, and may be viewed at any time, and
> taken away after the 16th of March next.

Derby Central Library, 'Derby Mercury'

Glossary and notes

This newspaper advertisement of 1799 mentions some of the fittings of a waterwheel.

30 The waterwheel at Arkwright's Cromford Corn Mill

Aerofilms Ltd

Glossary and notes

This photograph of an old waterwheel at Arkwright's Cromford Corn Mill shows how the drive was taken off by gear teeth on the rim of the wheel. This was better than driving by the axle.

Textile processes

31 Preparing cotton for spinning

Picking is that operation which prepares the cotton for carding, by opening the hard compressed masses in which it comes from the bales, and in separating it from seeds, leaves and other ADVENTITIOUS matter.

This operation was formerly, and is now in some degree, performed by beating the cotton with sticks on a square frame, across which are stretched cords, about the thickness of a goose quill, with intervals sufficient to allow the seeds, &c. to fall through. . . .

The operation of beating or batting by hand is now almost entirely superseded by the invention of machines, which have the advantage of more completely separating the dirt from the cotton; and consequently much manual labour in picking is avoided.

Carding is that operation in which the first rudiments of the thread are formed. It is performed by cylinders covered with wire cards, revolving, with considerable swiftness, in opposite directions, nearly in contact with each other, or under a kind of dome or covering, the under surface of which is covered with similar cards, whose teeth are inclined in a direction opposite to the cylinder. By this means the separation of almost every individual fibre is effected, every little knotty or entangled part is disengaged, and the cotton spread lightly and evenly over the whole surface of the last or finishing cylinder, from which it is stripped by a plate of metal, finely toothed at the edge, and moved in a perpendicular direction rapidly up and down by a crank.

The slight, but reiterated, strokes of this comb, acting on the teeth of the cards, detaches the cotton in a fine and uniform fleece; which being contracted by passing through a funnel and rollers, forms one endless and perpetual carding; which is interrupted or broken only when the can that receives it is completely filled.

Drawing and doubling, or passing three or four cardings at once through a system of rollers, by which they are made to COALESCE, is intended to dispose the fibres of the cotton LONGITUDINALLY, and in the most perfect state of parallelism, and at the same time, to correct any inequalities in the thickness of the cardings.

Roving is that operation by which the prepared cotton, as it comes from the drawing-frame is twisted into a loose and thick thread. In the state in which it comes from the drawing-frame it has little strength or TENACITY; and is received into similar deep cans from whence it was passed through the rollers. To enable it to support the operation of winding, it is again passed through a system of rollers, similar to those in the last machine, and received in a round conical can revolving with considerable swiftness. This gives the drawing a slight twisting, and converts it into a soft and loose thread, now called a roving, which is wound by hand upon a bobbin, by the smaller children of the mill, and then carried to the spinning, or twist-frame.

Glossary and notes

The work done in preparing cotton for the final stage of spinning is described carefully by a clergyman in an account of the Strutt Mill at Milford in the early 1800s. He was following the explanation of an expert workman. Four distinct processes are described: picking and batting; carding; drawing and doubling; roving. After this, the loosely wound bobbins of rovings were put on the spinning frames.

ADVENTITIOUS   accidental (here means rubbish).

COALESCE   combine in one.

LONGITUDINALLY   length wise.

TENACITY   firmness.

32 Cotton spinning in verse

First with nice eye emerging NAIADES cull
From leathery pods the vegetable wool;
With wiry teeth revolving cards release
The tangled knots, and smooth the ravell'd fleece;
Next moves the iron hand with fingers fine,
Combs the wide card, and forms the eternal line;
Slow, with soft lips, the whirling can acquires
The tender skeins, and warps in rising spires;
With quicken'd pace successive rollers move,
And these retain, and those extend the rove;
Then fly the SPOLES, the rapid axles glow,
And slowly CIRCUMVOLVES the labouring wheel below.

Glossary and notes

This poetic description was written by Dr Darwin—the grandfather of Darwin the biologist. We do not usually think of an industrial process as being a subject for poetry.

NAIADES   nymphs or young girls—here the factory girls.

SPOLES   spools.

CIRCUMVOLVES   turns around.

Mills

33 Derby silk mill

Derby Public Library

This illustration is of the Derby Silk Mill. The older part was built in 1702, and the larger building, on a row of arches, was completed in 1721. One of the Lombe brothers who built it had smuggled the plans for the machinery out of Italy. He later died mysteriously, poisoned in revenge, people said, by an Italian lady. It has quite a modern look about it, although it was already well-known in the 1770s as the Old Silk Mill. Many cotton manufacturers used it as a guide to how a textile factory should be built.

34 Belper
Mills from the air

Aerofilms Ltd.

Glossary and notes

This picture shows the complete range of late eighteenth- and early nine-teenth-century mills. Try to pick out the North Mill, South Mill, West Mill, and Round Mill, which was built on the 'Panopticon' plan. (Look up this word.) The very large block to the east was built about 100 years later. All but one of the early mills have been demolished recently, and replaced by new buildings. Only the North Mill still stands and is still in use.

35 Calver Mill, Derbyshire

Peak Park Planning Board

Glossary and notes

This mill was built in 1804 on the same site as a smaller one which was burnt down. The Owners were Gardom, Pares & Co (see extract 16, p. 19). The main block measures 170 ft by 38 ft.

4
Coal and
Iron

Introduction

To sink a shaft down to a seam of coal and provide all the equipment for extracting the coal was no simple task. The geological strata and its condition were unknown factors. The deeper the shaft had to be sunk, the greater the cost, to cope with such problems as water and ventilation. Only a wealthy man or a group of men with money, could afford to enter this industry and even then there were serious risks to face; but the ever increasing demand for coal and the financial rewards made the undertaking worth while.

The production of coal and iron

The Iron Industry has a long history and its origin and growth go back to the Middle Ages. During the eighteenth century there was an increasing demand for iron and the problem was to increase production by finding an alternative fuel to charcoal which would be cheaper. The letters which follow are all connected with the growth of the industry, the problems of supplies of iron, the opening of new coal mines and the development of coke smelting which was the result of Abraham Darby's research. In South Yorkshire the iron industry was in the hands of John Spencer of Cannon Hall, Barnsley, and Thomas Cockshutt of Underbank, Sheffield, who invested their wealth in the industry and eventually controlled all furnaces and forges within a radius of twenty miles of Barnsley.

36 A complaint about the quality of bar iron

London 17th Feb. 1742

Ben Dutton;

I have yours of the 11 & 19 now before me & I am glad you have ordered J. White to sink in Mrs Smith's land & have hopes of coming to the stone so soon. I wish Mr Marsden would give leave to sink in Mr Edmunds Ground . . . when he does give leave let J. White set on all the strength he can that we may have some in this blast, if you can agree with T. Broadbent . . . Pray mention what iron stone you suppose may be on Barnby Furnace hill & how long it may last . . . The stone in the new pitt in Stringers farm is better than in the others, so Mr Cotton shall not have it on any terms.

I am glad you like the nails. I shall mention the complaint to Mr Wortley & if Mr Cockshutt won't order the iron to be better slit I will send some to Mr Fell to slitt when the road is better . . .

J.D. is too hasty in promising $\frac{1}{2}$d per Thousand more, price for nails ordered before the next WEY . . . You do well to encourage the naylors. I shall give them a treat at my return as you promist & shall employ more than ever of Good hands if they will make good nails at the prices last given . . . Mr Cope writes that Mr Cotton was last friday & Saturday at Dodworth . . .

You must go on Sunday to Wortley forge & take Mr Cope with you & speak to Mr Thomas & the Slitter about the Slitting. Ask Mr Cope if he knew Mr. C——ns business at Dodworth.

To Mr Ben Dutton at Cannon Hall

John Spencer

Sheffield City Library, Spencer Stanhope MS 60489 (11)

Glossary and notes

This letter from Mr Spencer to his agent Ben Dutton concerns the sinking of new iron mines and expresses concern about the quality of iron for nails. Spencer is also very anxious to find out what Mr Cotton was doing at Dodworth. Cotton was also in the iron trade.

SLIT   the cutting of iron bars into suitable lengths for nail makers.

WEY   weigh.

37 Felling timber for charcoal

1748—27th Feb. Sheffield

I want a copy of Mr Wortley's lease of the Forges to yourself . . . I am thinking that if Mr Wortley sells any wood by the lump to a stranger that you are to take the CORDWOOD at the price fixed and to pay him money for the Cordwood delivered you by Mr Oates. If not Mr Wortley says he sells wood by the lump to any person that has an account with you, you'll be setting up with that person. So that you can force Mr Wortley to take down his woods himself & whether that be unfriendly or not he says you may judge.

I must desire you to give Mr Wortley a note under your hand that you'll pay the price for every Cord of wood to be so delivered to you unto Mr Wortley.

Yr Most humble servant
John Battie

Glossary and notes

In the mid-eighteenth century it was often a problem to get enough charcoal for the ironworks. In this letter John Battie wants John Spencer to make an offer to Mr Wortley rather than let the wood be sold to a rival.

CORDWOOD   branches of trees prepared for making into charcoal.

38 Leasing an ironworks

Frodsham
Chester   6 Oct 1779

Sir,

. . . . . as you say you will let your Furnace at Barnby upon fair and moderate terms. I will endeavour to point out what Repairs . . . are absolutely necessary for your Deliberation . . . I want to work it upon the principle Mr Walker's of Rotherham work theirs, that is with Pitcoal instead of charcoal . . . on acc^t of the Scarcity and Dearness of Cordwood, are worked so; and if the Pitcoal on your Estate shows chance to sink there will be a consumption of Seven Thousand Tons annually; that raised near the Glasshouse seems to be very suitable for the purpose. When Furnaces are worked on this Plan they are constantly going Winter and Summer; on acc^t of the great Scarcity of Water in Summer it will be necessary to build a Fire Engine to lift the Water from the Bottom of the Wheel into the Pond, to work it over and over again . . . there is at present a great Demand for Cannon Balls & I should wish to get to work as soon as possible. . . .

Sir, your most Obed^t Servt

Francis Dorset

Estimate of Repairs

A new Wheel, Troughs etc	£50	0	0
Cleaning the CUT below the Wheel	31	10	0
A new Hearth	31	10	0
Widening & enlarging the Furnace and new inside Walls	21	0	0
N.B. Coak Furnaces require to be made larger than Charcoal Furnaces.			
4 New Cilinders for Bellows w. Cranks Pipes and Gearing	200	0	0
Floodgates and Washer	10	0	0
A FIRE ENGINE to lift Water into the Pond	400	0	0
	£744	0	0

Sheffield City Library, Spencer Stanhope 60579, Letters on iron working 1778–1815

Glossary and notes

This letter is the result of a report from Mrs Darby about her father-in-law's successful discovery of the use of coke for smelting. It is from Francis Dorset a friend of John Spencer who was himself interested in the iron industry. Dorset would like to lease Barnby Furnace and this letter shows what was involved in converting a charcoal furnace to one using coke. The estimated cost was no small item in 1779.

FIRE ENGINE   a steam engine which worked on the Newcomen principle.

CUT   an outlet for water from a waterwheel to the river.

39 A discovery of new supplies of iron ore

Sir

There is a Discovery of a Bed of Iron Stone Breaking out in Silkstone Fall Wood in that part Now Going down and wich has every appearance of Being preferable to any ever discovered in any part of your Estate. It lies more than thirty yards above the other Bed but is superior ore and will be got at a very easy Rate as I think it will not cost more than fifteen pounds to lay it dry and also to Open the Foot or Fall of this ore and should supose there will be about 50 acres of it and if it proves according to every appearance there might either be a

Foundery Built where Silkstone Mill now stands or by Laying 280 yards of Railroad to Join the Original one to the Bason it would Cost 6s per tons Duty to the Bason and 5s Carriage . . . there is likewise a Bed of fine looking Coal near the Iron ore wich I think will prove very Valuable I think after it is got a little way into it will be about three foot thick and of Good quality. . . .

We seem to have a Good stock of Game left.

Barnby Furnace

14 April 1820

                    I am Sir
                        your very Humble Servant
George Hinchliffe

Glossary and notes

This letter is from George Hinchliffe, steward to John Spencer, giving details of the discovery of a bed of iron ore and coal in Silkstone Fall wood. He makes suggestions to Mr Spencer about the working of this find.

1826

The valuation of the wood etc. to go down in Silkstone Fall *being in the way of the iron stone pitts belonging to John Spencer Stanhope Esq.*

40 Valuation of wood to be cut to clear the ground to the ironstone pits

	£	s	d
To 31 Numbered Trees	35	7	6
To 59 Oak POLES	6	0	0
To 8 Ash Poles	1	3	6
To 31 Birch & Alder poles	1	8	0
To 63 fathoms of Barke at 4/4d per fathom	13	13	0
To 102 SHANKS AND TOPS	2	6	6
	£59:	6:	6

Glossary and notes

POLES   branches.

SHANKS AND TOPS   the ends cut off branches.

March 11th 1829;

Mr George Wilson and George Armitage to gether with Benjamin Mellor and Joshua Armatage, diged out a pit top belonging to Mr. Thomas Wilson Barnby Furnice in Silkstone Fall near to Mr Charlesworth's property.

Earth & Clay 1 yd 9 ins; Rage stone 1 yd 2 ft 6 ins; Blue Stone 6 ins; Blue Bind 6 ins; Stone or bank bed 1 ft.

Blue Bind 4 yds 2 ft 7 ins; Black scale 10 ins; Blue Bind 3 yds 2 ft; Coal 2 ft 9 ins; Spavin 1 yd; a lean ironstone bed 3 ins. . . .

41 Mine sinkers' report

Mine sinking was a specialised job and it was usual for sinkers to submit a report of the geological bands they found together with their thickness.

This is the report of the sinkers following the letter from George Hinchliffe to Mr Spencer.

42 Contract for sinking a mine

8 July 1833 *Silkstone Moor End Pit*
Agreement entered into by and between Benjamin Mellor agent to R. G. Clarke of the one part and George Hoyland, Thomas Watson and John Whollys of the other part being sinkers. That the said George Hoyland, Thomas Watson and John Whollys sink an Engine pit 8 feet diameter at £1:10s per yard while under the gin and to lade thayr own water to the number of 8 tubs per hour and likewise to find thayer own banks men and Drivers and afterwards to complete it down to what is commonly called the Silkstone bed of Coal under the Engine in two equal parts, the first at £2:10s per yard and the second part at £3 per yard, also put in pump stays, CRIBING, sheeting, water and air pipes and to compleate it in a workmanlike manner at the above prices and to be paid 10s for all water Cribs ordered in by the above B. Mellor.

It is further agreed that the said George Hoyland, Thomas Watson and John Wholly will sink a pit Commonly known by the name of by pit, also boar, put in Cribing sheeting, water and air pipes and compleat in a workmanlike manner down to the Silkstone Bed of Coal at £1:16 per yard and be paid for the water Cribs as above 9 ft 8 ins.

George Hoyland   X   his mark
Thomas Watson   X   his mark
J. Wholly   X   his mark.

Sheffield City Library, Clarke Papers CR144

Glossary and notes
It was usual to draw up a formal contract for sinking a mine and also the foundations for the pumping and winding engine. Notice that none of the three men involved in this contract was able to write his name.

CRIBING   support for the brickwork of a shaft while building.

SHEETING   a shaft lining.

DRIFT   an inclined underground roadway.

43 Expenses of sinking a mine at Alfreton, Derbyshire

Sinking an Engine Pit 50 yards at 50/- a yd	£125;0
Sinking a Coal Pit 50 yds at 30/-	75
A Gin for Sinking	50
Gin Ropes	20
Brick for Walling (70 yds at 8/- a yard)	28
Building a Shop for Blacksmith with materials	10
Sinking Gear, Blacksmith's Tools, Coal Picks etc	30

Preparing underground works, driving narrow drift	50
Laying and levelling 900 yards of Wagon way with	
Frame plates at 10/- a yard	450
A Steam Engine for Pumping water & drawing coal	700
Ten wagons at £8 each	80
Shaft frame with Pullies	30
3 Underground Wagons at 20/- each	3
Twelve Calfs of Sledges at 50/- each	3
Leading Materials & other Cartage	100
Two pairs of Machine Ropes	50
CONTINGENT Charges	46
Total Cost of Winning the Colliery	£1850

29 October 1814

Charles Brandling's Letter Book (Middleton Colliery), private collection of
P. Burgoyne Johnson

Glossary and notes

The cost of sinking a colliery shaft was no light undertaking for considerable expense and risk were involved. This should be compared with the contract for sinking Moor End Pit at Silkstone, extract 42.

CONTINGENT   unexpected.

44 Erecting a steam winding engine

Report from the Birmingham Gazette, 11th March 1776

a On Friday last, a steam engine constructed upon Mr Watt's new principles was set to work at Bloomfield Colliery, near Dudley, in the presence of . . . a number of scientific gentlemen whose curiosity was excited by so singular and so powerful a machine and whose expectations were fully gratified by the excellence of its performance. All the iron foundry parts (which are unparalleled for truth) were executed by Mr Wilkinson; the condenser with the valves, pistons and all the small work, at Soho. It made about 14 to 15 strokes per minute and is capable of working with one-fourth of the fuel that a common engine would require to produce the same quantity of power. The cylinder is 50 inches diameter and the length of the stroke is 7 feet.

L.T.C. Rolt, *James Watt*, Batsford, 1962

b Mr R. G. Clarke   Milton Ironworks
Silkstone Colliery   Elsecar
                                  2 Dec. 1835

Sir,
We now beg to hand you our terms for the Engine as requested; viz—high pressure with 13 in. Cylinder; Stroke of piston 3 feet, crosshead, guide rods, connecting rods, cranks and axle. Slide valve,

eccentric motion with boiler of 6 sq. ft. of Horse Power, grate bars, fire doors and frame. All erected at Silkstone Common for £315:0:0 One winding apparatus erected for £115:0:0

Graham & Co.

Science Museum, London

Glossary and notes

To supply coal for coking purposes and also to raise steam for the pumping engines, there was a need to develop mining on a larger scale. The old hand methods of winding were obsolete and steam engines were being installed.

A colliery sunk at Silkstone Common in 1833 had to be equipped with a pumping and a winding engine. Mr Clarke, the owner, wrote to the Milton Ironworks at Elsecar to enquire the price for a steam pumping engine and a winding engine.

The illustration shows you the type of engine used.

45 The cost of
mining coals at
Upholland Colliery

Coals got Jan 18th 1817 — £ s D

Wm Jackson	Scores 26½ at 2/11 ℗	3	17	3½
Mathew Worthington	25 at 2/11 ℗	3	12	11
Sherrington	15 at 2/9 ℗	2	1	3
Wm Lucas & Ashurst	6 at 2/8 ℗	"	16	"
		10	7	5½
Drynole Pit	Scores 72½	78	10	10
Odd Baskets for Fire Coals &c	Bas 58	2	8	4
Oven Cinders 200 at 3d/. ℗		3	"	"
	£	83	19	2
P^d for getting	Scores 72½	10	7	5½
P^d for Drawing Slack	9 at 1/2 ℗	"	10	6
P^d for winding Coals & Slack 81½ at 10 ℗		3	7	11
P^d for Taking off Coals & Slack 16 Days at 2/6 ℗		2	0	"
P^d for Driving ginn Horse 14 Days at 10 ℗		"	11	8
P^d for winding odd Baskets		0	2	6
P^d for Cutting 12 yards at 1/9 ℗		1	1	"
P^d for Burning 200 of Cinders		"	8	"
P^d Wm Liptrot for 13 Days work at 2/2 ℗		1	8	2
P^d A. Tinsley for 16 Days work at 2/. ℗		1	12	"
P^d John Winstanley for 6 Days work at 14^d ℗		"	7	"
P^d I. Whittle for 5 Days at 1/. ℗		"	5	"
P^d for Taking Props		"	5	"
P^d Letting the men Down to work		"	6	"
P^d for Candles 8 at 9^d ℗		"	6	"
P^d for Carting 2 Days at 10/. ℗		1	"	"
		23	18	2½

Lancashire Record Office, Coal Accounts for Upholland Colliery, 18 January 1817

46a Harrington Mill Pit Colliery, 1780

J. H. H. Holmes, 'A Treatise on the Coal Mines of Durham and Northumberland 1816'

b Hebburn Colliery, 1860

T. H. Hair, 'A Series of Views of the Collieries in the Counties of Northumberland and Durham, 1844'

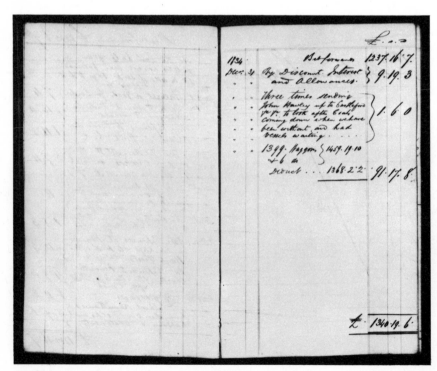

Sheffield City Libraries, Clarke Records CR8

48 Silkstone Colliery sales ledger, June 1822

Francis Cholmley	Barndsby Nr York	£12.12.0
Tim Rogerson	Royston	19. 0.0
Hood & Brown	Boroughbridge	14. 8.8
John Jewitt	Knottingley	40. 1.0
Geo. Kiersley	Ripon	15. 6.0
John Wales	Doncaster	12.12.0
Cooper & Parkin	Hull	10. 0.0
John Meek	York	76. 4.6
Luke Naylor	Doncaster	26.11.0
John Hyde	Gainsborough	12.12.0
G L Thompson	Sheriff Hutton Park, York	16. 4.0
James Chester	Thorne	11. 0.0
John Dobson & Co.	Selby	15. 0.0
Thomas Dawson	Driffield	7. 0.0

Leeds City Libraries

To coal owners and others: colliery materials on sale by private contract at Kexborough colliery, near Barnsley

1 Double Acting *steam engine* with Fly Wheel, nearly new, on Boulton and Watt's principle, 26 inch cylinder, 5 feet stroke, made by *Thompson* of Chesterfield

1 *Atmospheric steam engine* 28¾ inch Cylinder, 5 feet stroke with excellent Boiler and Fly Wheel

1 *Weighing machine* for Coal Waggons, Table 7 Feet by 5 Feet 7 inches to weigh 7 tons by Kitchen of Warrington

2 Sets *head gear* for Drawing Coals with *tipple doors* for loading and *hand gear* to Ditto complete

2 *Flat rope pullies*

5970 Feet Cast Iron *edge rails* for Waggon Road with Cross Plates, Chairs and stone sleepers complete

3981 Feet *waggon tram road rails* with cross plates and sleepers to ditto

4 Capital Smith's anvils

4 Smith's Bellows

21 Good Coal Waggons

A capital *timber bridge* adapted for crossing a *turnpike road*

A very good *gin, head gear* and *tipple doors*

A quantity of Brick Moulds and a large variety of other Articles adapted to Colliery Purposes.

Apply to *Mr. Timothy Marshall*, Darton, near Barnsley

'Sheffield Telegraph', January 1843

Glossary and notes

Sometimes collieries went bankrupt or the seams became too expensive to work. Then the colliery was closed and the equipment offered for sale, as in this case of Wilson's Colliery.

50 Getting rid of surplus coals

Wentworth 25 July 1770

My Lord

Inclosed I have sent your Lordship a Calculation what 100 DOZ. OF THE OLD LOW WOOD COALS would make more were they sent down to Kilnhurst. If the remaining part of the Summer turns out favourable, there seems a probability of getting clear of all Coals upon the Hill provided your Lordship would be agreeable to have as many sent down to the River as possible. Every Coal both there and at Elsecar would be sold in a Month's time if they were at the River side. There was never such a call for Coals upon the River since I can remember; the reason is so obvious; the Summers of late have been so exceeding wet that it has been impossible for People in the low Country that used to supply themselves by Land Carriage, to come at them anyway than by Water. The price at Rotherham is now 10/6 a Doz; delivered on Board; there is not the least doubt but that the price will continue all the Winter, as this Summer is so far advanced and no stock could be laid in by Land Carriage. If the remaining part of the Summer proves as wet as the [first] part, it would not be possible to get any great quantity even to Kilnhurst but if the vacant time betwixt Hay and Corn Harvest turns out dry, a great quantity might be got down in that time.

If your Lordship approves of having them sent down it would be the best way to insist upon the Tennants Carrying down as many as possible. There is a great quantity of Sope Ashes at Doncaster, I should imagine it might not be amiss to order them up to Kilnhurst for back carriage and then the same vessels that bring them up would take the Coals back—Your Lordship must consider that the Coals grows worse every year besides if they are rated at £3 a Doz; they lose 3d a Doz. each Year in their Value by Interest, therefore I should think it most advisable to quit them as soon as possible—A great inducement to send to the River is their not interferring with the Land Sale—There is now (if the Weather permits) a prospect of getting clear which if omitted may not happen again for a long time—They are getting forward to open the Colliery at Shafton as soon as possible, which will certainly take some Sale from us—If your Lordship determines to come into this Scheme you must please to aquaint me imediatly or the time will be past.

Yours sincerely
William Martin

The old Coals upon the Hill at Low Wood Colliery are set up at 81 Cubic Feet to the Doz; We know by experience that 100 Doz of them will set up to 85 Doz; at Kilnhurst, Parkgate measure, which is about 94½ Cubic Feet to the Doz; They would be sold at 10/6 the Parkgate doz;

85 Doz; at 10/6		£44:12:6
Cost; 100 Low Wood Doz; Carriage at 4/6	£22:10:0	
Wharfage and Stacking at 4d	1: 8:4	
Charge of 100 doz; at Kilnhurst	£23:18:4	
Which leaves for the Coals is better than 4/- a Doz.		£20:12:2

Sheffield City Library, Rockingham Papers R186–8

Glossary and notes

Before the introduction of canals and improved road transport, problems arose of how to dispose of surplus stocks of coal at the pithead. William Martin, Earl Fitzwilliam's agent, suggests ways of disposing of the coal by getting tenants on the estate to transport it to the river Don and bring back ashes for manure.

100 DOZ. OF THE OLD LOW WOOD COALS a dozen of coals is approximately two tons.

Customer relations

Sept. 9th		Dozens	Pulls	Price	£:s:d
Richard Rodes	Mexbro'	1		4/-	4:0
Thomas Best	Hoyland		4	4d	1:4
Mrs Hill	Jump		6	4d	2:0
Robert Beaumont	collier	2	7	13d	2:9½
William Carr	Elsecar	4		4/-	16:0
William Lockwood	Blacker		5	4d	1:8
John Hinchliffe	WOMBEL	1		4/-	4:0
Revd Mr Clayton	Bramton		6	4d	2:0
Widow Poels	Spittlehouse		6	4d	2:0
George Peace	Darfield	1	2	4/-	4:8
The Most Honourble Marquess of					
Rockingham delivered Swinton			6	4d	2:0
John Wigfield	Elsecar	4		4/-	16:0
Ben Gothard for the poor		1		4/-	4:0

51 Coals sold to local customers, Elsecar Colliery 1765

Wentworth Woodhouse Muniment, Sheffield City Library, A 1585 Sales Ledger

Glossary and notes

WOMBEL   the local spelling of Wombwell.

a York 28th March 1839
We have had complaints against your Coals lately—both from Town and Country—some have told me they would not believe they were Silkstone coals they are nearly as SWIFT as Haigh Moor and very dirty. I perceive the Cargoes differ but Tom Smith's Coals were very firm looking coals. . . .

Sam. Pierson

52 Customers' complaints

b Wakefield 28th Sept. 1839
. . . As you was not hear on friday i have sent to know when you could get me a Cargo of your Coals to Barnsley Canal end and what they would cost Brinding down as i shall be redy for them on Tusday or Wedensday to take them in. They are for Mr John Mountain of Boston it is the Sloop Bonington.

Yours

Direct to the White Bear Inn, Wakefield.   R Mountain

c Goole 30 May 1833
. . . I am sorry things are so bad at Goole, it will not be in my power to do you much good in the way of selling many coals. This fine weather causes vessels to go to the northward and as long as coals are so cheap there it has this bad effect upon us. So that to keep your pits at work and also your men, will it not be best to find out fresh channels for your coals in Brigg, Hull and Holderness. . . .

George Hawley

Sheffield City Library, Clarke Mss. 135G 133A

Not until the canal came did the coal market extend and as usual, some customers were ready to make complaints. These letters from coal merchants reveal details of the education of the writers, their opinion on coal and the state of the market.

SWIFT   quick-burning.

53 A cutler's advertisement

Sheffield City Libraries, 'The New York Daily Gazette', 1771

Glossary and notes

A copy of a Sheffield advertisement in the *New York Daily Gazette* for 1771. *Steel collars for children*, refers to the custom of placing a collar round the neck of negro slaves. You may be able to identify some of the instruments advertised.

THE

WORKING MAN:

A Weekly Record of Social and Industrial Progress.

ALL RIGHTS OF TRANSLATION AND REPRODUCTION ARE RESERVED.]   [REGISTERED FOR TRANSMISSION ABROAD.

VOL. I.—No. 5.]   SATURDAY, FEBRUARY 3, 1866.   { PRICE 2d. { STAMPED, 3d.

THE WORKSHOPS OF THE WORLD.

CUTTING BLADES   PUNCHING TEETH

GRINDING

SAW MAKING.

Sheffield Saw Manufacture.

THE saw is of great antiquity. It was known to the Egyptians and other early nations, and traces of its early use have been discovered in nearly every country where the arts and sciences have made the least progress. In England, Sheffield—the metropolis of our manufactures in steel—has had the saw-making almost entirely to itself, many hundreds of skilled and intelligent artisans being continually employed in this important branch of industry.

In former times, there was little variety in the shape of the saw, which in general appearance strongly resembled the *bow-saw* used by the carpenters. At the present day, however, the different kinds of saw—such as the *cross-cut-saw*, *pit-saw*, *frame-saw*, *ripping-saw*, *hand-saw*, *panel-saw*, *compass-saw*, and *such-saw*—are almost endless; the making of each kind of saw forming, as it

54a The range of iron and steelworks in Sheffield in the late nineteenth century

'Illustrated London News' 20 July 1899

b Forging
an axle

5
Transport

Canals

The construction of canals was essential to the expansion of industry. The south Yorkshire coalfield was unable to develop until a canal system was built to make easier the transport of heavy bulky goods, like coal, to areas demanding raw materials. The same problem faced the Duke of Bridgewater at Worsley and the need for improved transport was also a problem facing the Wedgwood family in the Potteries.

Canals proved to be erratic in their use. They were often short of water in a dry summer and frozen in a bad winter. Therefore attention began to be given to transport by locomotive, first from collieries to canals or ports, and then to the gradual growth of a national system of railways which covered the needs of passengers as well as goods.

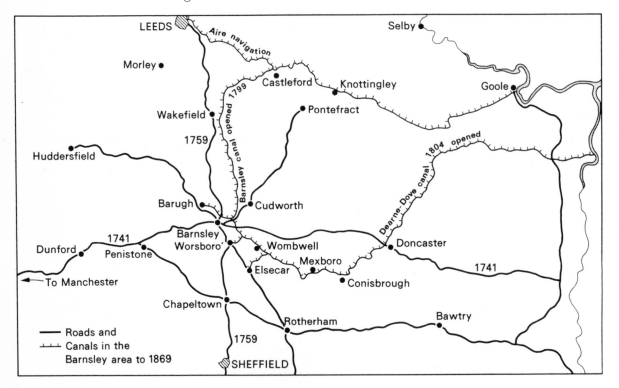

55 Inland shipping

Derby Central Library, 'Derby Mercury'

56

One of the biggest problems the textile industry had to face in the early days was transport. The raw materials had to be brought to the mill and the manufactured articles had to be sent to the customers.

Canal transport was often used, and navigable rivers made it possible for small sea-going ships to sail quite a long way inland. This sort of paragraph appeared regularly in the *Derby Mercury*. First comes the name of the coaster, then the master's name, and then the cargo.

56 Transport costs

It is with reluctance but necessity obliges me to inform you the present rates of your Freight by Canal to and from Derby are so low that they will not cover the expences. Have lately been oblig'd to advance my servants' pay who work the Boats and owing to the high price of Provisions for both Men and Horses they want a further advance which shall be oblig'd to give them. I trust the small extra charge to you will be consider'd reasonable. Namely all Goods to or from Derby to be 3*s* 0*d* pr. Cwt. for Freight with 3*d*. pr. Cwt. for Cartage on all goods to commence at the end of the ensuing GENERAL STOPPAGE about the 21st Inst.

Quoted in Fitton and Wadsworth, 'The Strutts and the Arkwrights', 1958

Glossary and notes

Strutts of Belper got much of their raw cotton from London via Gainsborough. From there it was taken by smaller boats to Derby, and then by waggon to Belper. Some was brought all the way from London by canal. Some came from Liverpool. Sometimes increased transport costs had to be faced. In May 1825 Holts, the carriers, wrote this letter to Strutts.

GENERAL STOPPAGE   the canals were being closed for cleaning.

57 Damage in transit

The following Nos. of Sea Island Cotton by F. & S. are come in so shameful a condition that we must charge someone with the damage. The ropes are broken, the bags burst, & the Cotton strewed about in a way we never saw before. The boatmen from Gainsbro' say they received them in that state—it will be well if they can prove it because then if you can prove the delivery in a good state, the damage is fixed on the Carrier between London and Gainsbro'. Please to examine into it and inform us as soon as may be.

Quoted in Fitton and Wadsworth, 'The Strutts and the Arkwrights', 1958

Glossary and notes

This extract shows some of the risks of transport. It is from a letter written by Strutts to their broker, or agent, in London, in February, 1826.

58 The benefit of canals

The cottage, instead of being covered with miserable thatch, is now secured with a substantial covering of tiles or slates, brought from the distant hills of Wales or Cumberland. The fields, which before were barren, are now drained, and, by the assistance of manure, conveyed on the canal toll-free, are cloathed with a beautiful verdure. Places which rarely knew the use of coal are plentifully supplied with that essential article upon reasonable terms: and, what is still of greater public utility, the monopolizers of corn are prevented from exercising their infamous trade.

Thomas Pennant, 'The Journey from Chester to London', 1779

Glossary and notes
The traveller, Thomas Pennant, is writing here about the Trent and Mersey Canal, also known as the Grand Trunk. It could have been written of any English canal.

59 Canal and tramroad

Waterways Museum, Stoke Bruerne

Glossary and notes

Long before the true railways began, waggon-ways or tramroads were in use. On these, horses drew trucks along a cast-iron track. The picture shows a barge being loaded from the tramroad at Little Eaton Wharf on the Derby Canal. The track was laid in 1795 and the photo was taken shortly before it was closed in 1908. It was about six miles long and was used to bring coal from local pits to the canal.

60 Canal and road

Nottingham Public Libraries, Local History Library

Glossary and notes

Notice in this early nineteenth-century watercolour the typical hump-backed canal bridge and the turnpike gate across the road.

61 Report on a proposed canal

16 March 1793

The Collieries in the Vicinity of Rotherham have been decreasing for several years past and are now become so much reduced both in number and produce that the Counties of York and Lincoln have experienced a loss of that supply which they receive by means of the River Dun.

To provide an adequate remedy to an evil so serious and alarming, the attention of the River Dun Company was naturally turned to that valuable tract of country abounding in Coal of the best quality ... extending ... through the estates of the Earl Fitzwilliam, Lord Strafford, Lady Bute and others to the productive collieries in the vicinity of Barnsley, and particularly to a place called Silkstone, in which neighbourhood there are found some of the finest beds of Coal in the Kingdom.

For this purpose they set on foot the scheme of a Navigable Canal from the River Dun Navigation-cut in the parish of Swinton, to approach the above mentioned estates to run through the parish of Barnsley, up to the parish of Silkstone with a branch to communicate with the Collieries near Haigh Bridge; and that the County of Lincoln ... might have the best access to the supply, and at the same time obtain a more speedy and cheap conveyance of its grain products to a very populous part of the West Riding of the County of York. ...

... that the Aire and Calder Company should apply to Parliament for leave to form a Canal from Wakefield by Barnsley up to Barnby Bridge in the vicinity of Silkstone, with a collateral cut to Haigh Bridge which Canal is to be called the Barnsley Canal. ...

The Dearn and Dove and Barnsley Canal will ... afford a union betwixt the River Dun and Calder and a new approach to Wakefield, Halifax, Leeds and other places situated on the Aire and Calder. ...

Sheffield City Libraries, Wentworth Woodhouse Muniments Handbill 14

Glossary and notes

It was impossible to develop the South Yorkshire coal and iron field without some improvement in transporting heavy goods. There were two ways in which this was carried out, the first by constructing a system of canals and the second by the development of the railway, which was both quicker and easier than the canal.

This report on the proposed canal in 1793 is taken from a handbill printed in 1793 to advertise the advantages this canal would bring. The proposed cut through Haigh Bridge never took place because there was a serious problem of constructing a tunnel about one mile in length to the Aire and Calder. The canal terminated at Barnby Bridge in Cawthorne.

Sheffield City Libraries.

Railways

Willington
Newcastle on Tyne
11 October 1813

Dear Sir,

In reply to your favour of the 6th instant I shall at all times have great pleasure in affording to his Grace the Duke of Portland ... every information in my power respecting the new mode of leading our Coals by Steam Engines instead of Horses.

The Engine which is used is considered of four horses Power of Trevithicks invention being the most powerful we have in use at present and is made by Fenton, Murray and Wood of Leeds . . . and costs £380 including £30 paid to Trevithick for his patent right.

The Engine is so constituted that by the operating power of Cranks which turn a Cogged wheel working in Metal Coggs cast upon one side of the Rail laid and used as the Railway.

At Leeds they have been daily at work for some time back leading their Coals in this way and as their Road is perfectly level their Engines take with great ease 24, twenty Boll wagons loaded at a time—each wagon weighs with its contents about $3\frac{1}{2}$ Tons, making together an aggregate weight of 84 Tons. When the Machine is lightly loaded it can be propelled at the rate of 10 Miles an hour; but when properly loaded is calculated to go at the rate from $3\frac{1}{2}$ to 4 Miles an hour upon a level way. . . .

Should the length of the lead from his Lordship's Concerns in Ayrshire be considerable I have no doubt that an immense saving will be made by the adoption of Mr Blenkinsop's new method. . . .

Yours most respectfully
John Walton

Mr Bailey
Agent to the D. of Portland.

64 More interest in the early railways

Middleton Colliery
5 October 1814

Sir,
I beg leave to forward to you answers to the Queries regarding the Steam Machine for Iron Railways for the information of Sir John Sinclair Bart.

Query 1 By whom were they first invented or tried?

Answer By the undersigned—Patent granted April 1811.

Query 2 How long have they been at work and at what places?

Answer At Middleton Colliery near Leeds belonging to Charles John Brandling Esq. since June 1812, also at Orrell Colliery near Wigan in Lancashire; Kenton & Coxlodge Collieries near Newcastle.

Query 3 What is the original expense?

Answer The Steam Carriage with two 8 inch Cylinders will cost £400.

Query 5 What weight do they draw?

Answer The engines at present in use convey 100 Tons.

Query 7 At what rate might they be made to go an hour?

Answer When the carriage is lightly loaded it travels at the rate of 10 miles an hour but when loaded with 27 Coal Wagons each loaded with $3\frac{1}{2}$ tons it is propelled on a dead level at the rate of $3\frac{1}{2}$ miles an hour. The machine weighs 5 Tons.

Query 8 Could they be made applicable to public Roads? for instance from London to Edinburgh if Iron Railways were made along the sides of the Road?

Answer Yes,—the only inconvenience would be in going through large towns to remedy which wheels might be made to run on the pavement as well as the Rail Road and the machine taken through the Town by Horses.

The locomotive Engine of 8 inch Cylinder is performing the work of 16 Horses in 12 Hours and as the annual expenses does not exceed £200 the savings will therefore be £1200 at least by the use of this machine invention in a year.

The Steam carriage was at work last winter at Middleton night and Day and was not impeded during the great falls of snow.

I am Sir,
Your Obid. Servt.
John Blenkinsop

Charles Brandling Letter Book, private collection of P. Burgoyne Johnson

Glossary and notes

John Blenkinsop with the assistance of Matthew Murray developed Trevithick's idea of a locomotive to pull trains of wagons from Middleton colliery to the river Aire at Leeds. This development of a railway proved to be far quicker and cheaper than using horses. These two letters, one to the Duke of Portland's agent from John Walton, one of the partners in the colliery, gives an account of the cost of operating it.

The second letter is from Blenkinsop himself replying to Sir John Sinclair's agent on the problems and possibility of building a railway from London to Edinburgh almost 30 years before such a railway was constructed.

65 Objections to the Stockton to Darlington Railway

Mr Foster
Queen's Head
Newcastle on Tyne

5th February 1819

A set of Merchants and Speculators are endeavouring to obtain an Act of Parliament to enable them to make a Railway from Stockton to Darlington. . . . The said Speculators being a few individuals who hope to be beniffitted at the expense of the country, as the measure is not for the general benifit, and will . . . prove disastrous to those concerned. The said projected Railway will very materially injure the highly cultivated district through which it is proposed to carry it and cut up and intersect the enclosures which are now laid out at much expense . . . for the purpose of agriculture and good management as besides the Darlington line, which passes for nearly two miles through my property, a Branch is intended to go to Piercebridge . . . through the best part of my property. It is well known that the damage done, in making roads . . . besides the depridations . . . committed upon the crops and other property of Landowners, by the trespassing of Cattle and people employed in the traffic of the said Railway. And it does not meet with the concurrence of the Landed Proprietors over whose property it is proposed to carry it, on the contrary it is almost universally opposed by them. . . .

Matthew Cully

Northumberland County Record Office, Cully MSS. Folder 35

66 Threat to the railway company 31 May 1829

I am extremely sorry to be obliged to give you notice that if you do not discontinue the fire Engines which take waggons or as they are sometimes called the Iron Horses along your Railway from Stockton to Darlington . . . I shall take such steps for the Publick good that I may be advised. . . . Within this last fortnight two accidents have happened which might have terminated in the death of the parties and one person who was thrown on the road is now labouring under the effects of the fall and should any serious consequences follow I shall feel myself bound to prosecute as far as the law will allow.

Tomlinson MSS. Newcastle Central Reference Library

Glossary and notes

The railway was not accepted by everyone as a desirable method of transport. Both Matthew Cully and Lord Darlington, who were land owners affected by the construction of the Stockton to Darlington railway, objected to the Members of Parliament in the hope that they would refuse to vote in favour of a Bill to build the line. Even after the success of the Rainhill Trials of 1829, William Chaytor wrote a bitter letter of complaint to the Committee of the Stockton and Darlington Railway.

67 An early railway ticket

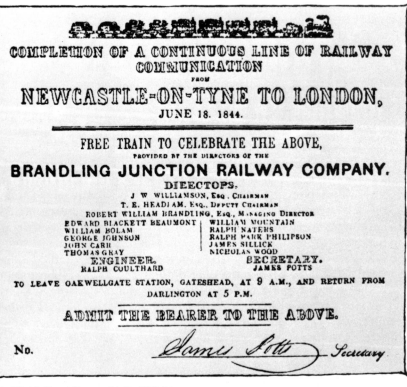

Sheffield City Library, M.D. 990 M

at 9.10 p.m., on Saturdays only.

Manchester, Sheffield, and Lincolnshire Line.

BARNSLEY TO PENISTONE, SHEFFIELD, LONDON, AND (via Manchester, Sheffield, and Lincolnshire) MANCHESTER.

UP.		WEEK-DAYS.				SUNDAYS.	
	1 2 3	1 & 2	1 2 3	1&2	1 2 3	1 2 3	1 2 3	1 2 3
Barnsley......dep	6 25	9 25	12 20	4 32	6 25	7 30	4 30	7 55
Dodworth	6 34	9 34	12 30	4 41	6 34	7 40	4 40	8 5
Silkstone...........	6 40	9 40	12 36	4 47	6 40	7 48	4 48	8 13
Penistone	6 50	9 50	12 46	4 57	6 50	8 0	5 0	8 23
Sheffield	8 15	10 50	1 23	...	7 30	9 5	5 40	...
London, K. Cross	3 30	3 5	6 0	...	3 45	7 45	10 15	...
MANCHESTER...arr	8 25	11 30	2 10	6 0	8 0	9 40	...	10 0

LONDON TO SHEFFIELD, MANCHESTER, PENISTONE AND BARNSLEY.

DOWN.		WEEK-DAYS.				SUNDAYS.	
London, K. Cross	...		10 0	12 0	2 45	...	...	...
Sheffield	6 10	9 35	2 30	4 40	6 45	7 30	...	7 55
Manchester..........	6 5	9 50	1 50	5 0	6 30	7 0	3 35	
	1 2 3	1&2	1 2 3	1&2	1&2	1 2 3	1 2 3	1 2 3
Penistone.............	7 45	10 45	3 28	5 55	8 5	8 34	5 15	8 45
Silkstone............	7 54	10 54	3 37	6 4	8 15	8 44	5 25	8 55
Dodworth	8 0	11 0	3 43	6 10	8 21	8 50	5 34	9 2
BARNSLEY ......arr	8 8	11 8	3 51	6 18	8 30	9 0	5 44	9 15

A Market Train leaves Barnsley, on Saturdays only, at 9.30 p.m. for Dodworth, Silkstone, and Penistone.

MIDLAND LINE.

BARNSLEY TO LONDON, SHEFFIELD, DERBY, VIA CUDWORTH.

UP.		WEEK-DAYS.			SUNDAYS	
	1, 2, 3	1 & 2	1 2 3	Gov	Gov	Gov
CUDWORTH (for Barnsley	7 4	9 25	2 0	6 12	8 24	4 2
Darfield	7 13	9 35	2 11	6 22	8 13	4 14
Wath and Bolton	7 21	9 40	2 17	6 27	8 18	4 20
Swinton	7 27	9 47	2 23	6 33	8 25	4 25
Masbro' for Rotherham..	7 45	10 3	2 42	6 53	8 40	4 40
Sheffield	8 5	10 20	3 0	7 15	9 5	4 55
Derby	10 0	11 55	4 35	9 0	11 0	6 45
LONDON Euston Square...	3 50	--	9 50	--	6 15	--
LONDON King's Cross...	3 50	3 50	--	--	--	--

LONDON TO BARNSLEY VIA CUDWORTH.

DOWN.		WEEK-DAYS.			SUNDAYS.	
	Gov	1 & 2	Gov	Gov	Gov	1&2	Gov
LONDON Kings Cross	—	--	7 20	—	—	—	aft.
LONDON Euston Sq.	—	—	—	—	10 0	—	—
Derby	6 0	10 35	1 25	—	7 0	3 45	6 15
Sheffield	7 45	11 55	2 55	7 20	8 20	5 0	7 40
Masbro' (Rotherham	8 0	12 13	3 19	7 42	8 50	5 16	8 0
Swinton	8 15	12 25	3 33	7 57	9 3	5 34	8 16
Wath and Bolton ...	8 20	—	3 39	8 4	9 9	—	8 23
Darfield	8 25	—	3 44	8 9	9 15	—	8 28
CUDWORTH (Barnsley	8 35	12 40	3 53	8 19	9 26	5 52	8 40

BARNSLEY TO WAKEFIELD AND LEEDS VIA CUDWORTH.

DOWN.		WEEK-DAYS.			SUNDAYS.	
	Gov	1 & 2	Gov	Gov	Gov	Gov	Gov
CUDWORTH (Barnsley	8 35	12 40	3 53	8 19	9 26	5 52	8 40
Royston & Notton...	8 44	—	4 4	8 28	9 34	—	8 50
Oakenshaw.........	9 0	12 56	4 15	8 41	9 45	6 10	9 0
WAKEFIELD..........	9 10	1 20	4 20	8 45	—	—	—
Normanton	9 8	1 3	4 25	8 50	—	—	9 6
LEEDS ....arr	9 45	1 30	5 5	9 30	10 25	6 55	9 45

LEEDS AND WAKEFIELD TO BARNSLEY VIA CUDWORTH.

UP.		WEEK-DAYS.			SUNDAYS	
	1 2 3		1 2 3	Gov	Gov	Gov
LEEDS ....dep.	6		1	55	5 7	0	3 0
Normanton.............	6 28	8 47	1 32	5 34	7 26	3 29
WAKEFIELD.............	6 40	8 58	—	5 37	—	—
Oakenshaw.............	6 41	8 59	1 46	5 48	7 41	3 43
Royston and Notton......	6 56	—	—	6 3	7 53	3 52
CUDWORTH (Barnsley) ar.	7 4	9 25	2 0	6 12	8 24	4 2

'The Barnsley Chronicle', 19 May 1866

69 The opening of the Sheffield-Rotherham Railway

The ceremony of opening the Sheffield and Rotherham Railway took place on Wednesday last, on which occasion Sheffield certainly poured forth its thousands of inhabitants to witness the proceedings. At Rotherham the bells rang merry peals from an early hour throughout the day. In Mr Badger's garden [he was the solicitor to the Company] ... were placed pieces of cannon which were fired at intervals during the day especially on the arrival and departure of each train. At Sheffield the entrance to the station was ornamented ... The arrangement was that the first train should start at ten o'clock from Sheffield and ... should leave Rotherham to come back at one o'clock. Some delay was occasioned by the late arrival of Earl Fitzwilliam and a party from Wentworth House.

At eight minutes before eleven o'clock the first train consisting of two sets of carriages and preceded by two engines the London and the Victory started from Sheffield, the band playing 'God save the Queen'. The carriages proceeded at a comparatively gentle speed and arrived at Rotherham station in nineteen minutes. ...

The engines of which there are at present three were made by Messrs Robert Stephenson and Company of Newcastle-on-Tyne and are very handsome specimens. The carriages, of which those called first class are exceedingly beautiful and well fitted up, were manufactured by Messrs Richard Melling and Company of Green Hayes near Manchester. We believe great praise is due to the engineer F. Swanwick Esq. for the taste he has displayed in bringing the work to its present state of perfection. It must be remembered that the work is not yet by far completed.

'Doncaster, Nottingham and Lincoln Gazette', 3 November 1838

70a Travel tokens

Sheffield City Library

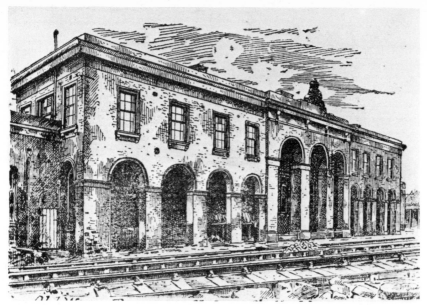

Sheffield City Library, Newspaper cuttings relating to Sheffield

c The first train
goes over the Wicker
Arches, Sheffield

Museum and Art Gallery, Rotherham

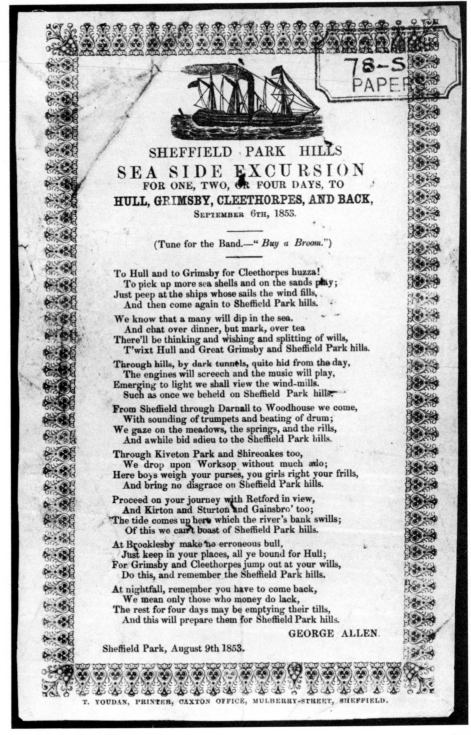

SHEFFIELD PARK HILLS
SEA SIDE EXCURSION
FOR ONE, TWO, OR FOUR DAYS, TO
HULL, GRIMSBY, CLEETHORPES, AND BACK,
SEPTEMBER 6TH, 1853.

(Tune for the Band.—"*Buy a Broom*.")

To Hull and to Grimsby for Cleethorpes huzza!
   To pick up more sea shells and on the sands play;
Just peep at the ships whose sails the wind fills,
   And then come again to Sheffield Park hills.

We know that a many will dip in the sea.
   And chat over dinner, but mark, over tea
There'll be thinking and wishing and splitting of wills,
   T'wixt Hull and Great Grimsby and Sheffield Park hills.

Through hills, by dark tunnels, quite hid from the day,
   The engines will screech and the music will play,
Emerging to light we shall view the wind-mills.
   Such as once we beheld on Sheffield Park hills.

From Sheffield through Darnall to Woodhouse we come,
   With sounding of trumpets and beating of drum;
We gaze on the meadows, the springs, and the rills,
   And awhile bid adieu to the Sheffield Park hills.

Through Kiveton Park and Shireoakes too,
   We drop upon Worksop without much ado;
Here boys weigh your purses, you girls right your frills,
   And bring no disgrace on Sheffield Park hills.

Proceed on your journey with Retford in view,
   And Kirton and Sturton and Gainsbro' too;
The tide comes up here which the river's bank swills;
   Of this we can't boast of Sheffield Park hills.

At Brooklesby make no erroneous bull,
   Just keep in your places, all ye bound for Hull;
For Grimsby and Cleethorpes jump out at your wills,
   Do this, and remember the Sheffield Park hills.

At nightfall, remember you have to come back,
   We mean only those who money do lack,
The rest for four days may be emptying their tills,
   And this will prepare them for Sheffield Park hills.

GEORGE ALLEN.

Sheffield Park, August 9th 1853.

T. YOUDAN, PRINTER, CAXTON OFFICE, MULBERRY-STREET, SHEFFIELD.

Words under the music:

O, in eigh-teen hun-dred and for-ty one Me cor-du-roy bree-ches I— put on, Me— cor-du-roy bree-ches I put on to work up-on the rail-way the rail-way. I'm wear-y of the rail-way, O, poor Pad-dy works on the rail-way.

O, in eighteen hundred and forty one
Me corduroy breeches I put on,
Me corduroy breeches I put on
To work upon the railway, the railway.

Chorus

I'm weary of the railway,
O, poor Paddy works on the railway.

O, in eighteen hundred and forty two
From Hartlepool I moved to Crewe
And I found myself a job to do
A workin' on the railway, the railway.

O, in eighteen hundred and forty three
I broke me shovel across me knee
And went to work for the company
On the Leeds and Selby railway, the railway.

O, in eighteen hundred and forty four
I landed on the Liverpool shore;
Me belly was empty me hands were sore
With workin' on the railway, the railway.

O, in eighteen hundred and forty five
When Daniel O'Connell he was alive,
When Daniel O'Connell he was alive
And workin' on the railway, the railway.

O, in eighteen hundred and forty six
I changed me trade from carrying bricks,
I changed me trade from carrying bricks.
To work upon the railway, the railway.

O, in eighteen hundred and forty seven
Poor Paddy was thinking of going to heaven,
Poor Paddy was thinking of going to heaven
And workin' on the railway, the railway.

Words: Ewan MacColl, 'The Shuttle and Cage', London, n.d. (1954), p. 20.
Tune: W. B. Whall, 'Sea Songs and Shanties', Glasgow, 1963 (first published
1910), p. 67. The song has been recorded by Ewan MacColl ('Men at Work',
Topic TPS166)

The navvies were originally the 'navigators' who built canals. The same men, using picks and shovels, were employed on railway construction. The song probably originated with Irish railway navvies, was popular also as a sea shanty, and is still current in the oral tradition in Ireland.

73 Railway excursion, 1841

In 1841 one of the first excursions organised in the country was run from Sheffield to Derby. The fares were 7s first class, 5s second class, 4s third class. The latter consisted of open trucks.

. . . 2,000 brave souls embarked on this great adventure. They were conveyed in one long train of 45 trucks and carriages pulled by five engines . . . The only casualty occuring, apart from several hats being blown away, was . . . a worthy gentleman who excitedly got up from his seat before the train came to a standstill in Wicker Station and fell overboard.

'Sheffield Telegraph' 30th June 1923

74 Railway Act 1844

Be it enacted that . . . all passenger Railway Companies which shall have been incorporated by any act of the present session; or which shall hereafter be incorporated . . . shall by means of one train at the least to travel along their railway from one end to the other of each trunk, branch or junction line belonging to them . . . once at the least on every week day, except Christmas Day and Good Friday (such exception not to extend to Scotland) provide for the conveyance of Third Class passengers to and from the terminal and other ordinary passenger stations of the railway. . . .

Such train shall start at an hour to be from time to time fixed by the Directors. . . .

Such train shall travel at an average speed of not less than twelve miles an hour for the whole distance . . . including stoppages.

The carriages in which passengers shall be conveyed by such train shall be provided with seats and shall be protected from the weather. The fare or charge shall not exceed one penny for each mile travelled.

Statutes at Large vol. xxvi p. 451

6
Child Labour
and Apprenticeship

Introduction

Apprentices were sent by their parents to live and work with a master craftsman and to be taught a trade. The parents had to pay a premium to the master. The apprentice was looked after by the master but was not paid. Before factories became common it was quite normal for children as young as six or seven to work at some job (see p. 77). (see p. 77) Parents did not often apprentice daughters, though most of the ordinary workers in textile mills were women and children. Parish children were children who for some reason had no one to look after them, perhaps because they were orphans. They were under the care of the Parish officials. If they were apprenticed, they were called Parish apprentices or pauper apprentices.

After the coming of the factory system, hundreds of parish children were apprenticed to factory owners. They were still parish apprentices, but were also called factory apprentices. They lived in an apprentice-house at the mill and were fed and clothed by the employers but were not paid wages.

The use of parish apprentices to work in factories began to end after 1802 and factory owners hired children who were living at home with their parents. These were sometimes called 'free' children, and they were paid wages, but they might still be roughly treated at work and it was 1833 before an effective law was made about child workers.

The original apprenticeship system continued in the skilled trades throughout the period. The apprenticing of individual Parish children to anyone who would take them also continued.

75 An indenture

Derbyshire County Record Office

Glossary and notes

Hannah Brown was an orphan who was apprenticed by the parish authorities
of Alfreton, to Daniel Morrell, in 1788. This is the indenture.

76 A discharge certificate

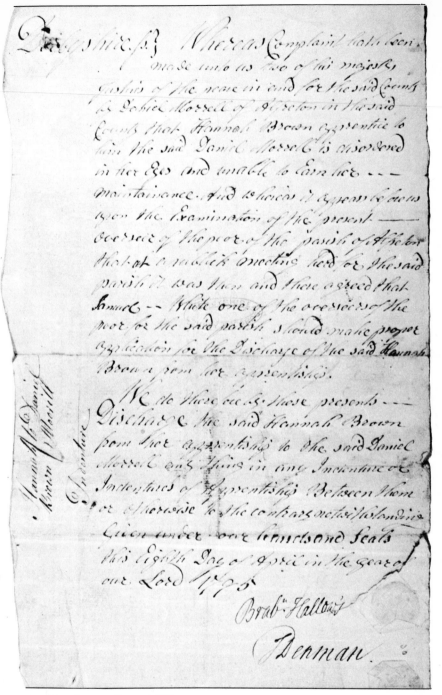

Derbyshire County Record Office

Glossary and notes

On the back of the indenture this discharge certificate is written. Occasionally apprentices were discharged at their own request because of ill-treatment. In this case it is the master who has asked for the discharge.

An Apprentice & having been misused by his master by not being
provided with proper clothes and refusing to wash for him.

This business was heard by Mr Hurt & Mr Strutt and they find
that Francis Rice the Apprentice is ill clothed & has not clean linen
as he ought to have & do adjudge Peter May the Master to pay the
expenses (8/-) telling him at the same time that if he does not clothe
and wash for the Boy in a proper manner & also teach him his trade
he will be discharged & a distress made for the premium.

Belper Petty Sessions Records

77 An apprentice 'misused'

Glossary and notes

Even an ordinary apprentice who had relatives to help him might not be well
treated by his master. On 25 January 1831 this case was heard in Belper
Petty Sessions Court, against Peter May of Belper, hatter. The charge was
brought by John Rice, on behalf of Francis Rice.

An apprentice being guilty of several misdemeanours in his service
particularly by absenting himself and lying out of nights.

Committed to the House of Correction to hard labour for six weeks
by F. Hurt & J. Radford Jun[r] Esquires.

Belper Petty Sessions Records

78 An apprentice misbehaves

Glossary and notes

Apprentices might also be at fault, however! On 28 May 1831 Francis Rice,
the apprentice, was brought to court by Peter May.

79 A runaway apprentice

Apprentice Absconded.

RUN AWAY, from Cromford Cotton Mills,
in the County of Derby; JOHN FLINT, by Trade a
Joiner; he is a stout young Man, about 20 Years of Age,
Red Hair, and has a Mole on his Face.
Whoever will give Information to Mr. RICHARD
ARKWRIGHT, of Cromford aforesaid, of the Person
that Employs the above Apprentice, shall be handsomely
rewarded for their Trouble.

Derby Central Library, 'Daily Mercury'

Glossary and notes

Sometimes an apprentice would break the agreement made for him, and run
away, to get a paid job. This sort of notice was common in newspapers of the
time.

80 An attempt at protection, 1784

Resolved. That it is the Opinion of this Court, that it is highly expedient for the Magistrates in this County to Refuse their Allowance to all Indentures of Parish Apprentices, who shall be Bound to Owners of Cotton Mills or other Manufactories, in which Children are obliged to Work in the Night or more than Ten Hours in a Day.

And it is Ordered that this Resolution shall be Communicated to the Clerks of the Peace for the Counties of Chester, Stafford, Flint, Denbigh, Derby, York and Westmorland and that the same shall be published in the Manchester and Liverpool Newspapers

By Order of the Court
James Taylor
Deputy Clerk of the Peace.

Lancashire Record Office, Quarter Sessions Orders, 1784

Glossary and notes

This resolution was passed by the Justices of Peace for Lancashire concerning the abuse of child labour in 1784. The Justices knew what conditions were like and were anxious to prevent the practice spreading. Like the early Factory Acts this had little effect.

Conditions and treatment

81 Kind treatment at Cressbrook Mill 1824

Two or three hundred children are employed at Cresbrook, and reside in the spacious buildings adjoining. The first feeling this consciousness awakens is compassion, that so many human beings, at that tender age when all the fond affections are first implanted, should be separated from their natural connexions, and thrown upon strangers, to whom they can have no other claim, or who feel no other tie towards them, than that of interest; but an acquaintance with this large, and well-organized family, will soften those feelings, and rectify their erroneous conclusions. . . .

At Cresbrook-mill constant and regular industry is enforced, but no unnatural labour. Their hours of work and necessary relaxation are kindly and judiciously arranged; the former never exceeding what ought to be exacted from those in their station of life and of their tender age; their food is of the best quality, and amply dispensed; they have eight hours uninterrupted sleep, in comfortable beds and airy rooms; the utmost decorum is maintained between the boys and girls; but if a brother and sister be amongst the number, the affectionate relationship is kindly encouraged; the relatives of the children are allowed to come to the House, where they are hospitably entertained, and permitted to remain a suitable time, according to their own behaviour, and the distance from whence they came; personal cleanliness is inculcated and enforced with the most scrupulous attention. On particular Festivals, and in fine weather, the children attend Tideswell Church, the distance of three miles; but in Winter they have a Sunday-school, and the service of the Church of England read to them, in one of their large rooms; the boys and girls having each separate apartments,—such are their duties.

Mary Sterndale, 'Vignettes of Derbyshire', 1824

Glossary and notes

In this extract a lady describes Cressbrook Mill which she visited in 1824. Cressbrook was one of the 'good' mills, employing parish apprentices.

INTEREST   concern for material welfare only.

82 Mr Arkwright's children

August 22

In the evening I walked to Cromford & saw the Children coming from their work out of one of Mr. Arkwright's Manufactories. I was glad to see them look in general very healthy and many with fine, rosy, complexions. These children had been at work from 6 or 7 o'clock this morning, & it was now near or abt. 7 in the evening. The time allowed them for resting is at 12 o'clock 40 minutes during which time they dine. One of them, a Boy of 10 or 11 years of age told me his wages were 3s 6d a week, & a little girl said Her wages were 2s 3d a week.

August 23

We went to Church at Cromford where is a Chapel built abt. 3 years & ½ ago by Mr. Arkwright. On each side the Organ a gallery in which about 50 Boys were seated. These children are employed in Mr. Arkwright's work in the week-days, and on Sundays attend a school where they receive education. They came to Chapel in regular order and looked healthy & well & were decently cloathed & clean. They were attended by an Old Man their School Master. To this school girls also go for the same purpose, and alternately with the Boys go to Church. . . .

Greig, ed. 'The Farington Diary', 1922

Glossary and notes

Even the paid children in some mills were 'brought up' as much by their employer as by their actual parents. Joseph Farington R.A. passed through Cromford in 1801, with three friends on a trip to Scotland, 'having a Landaulet & two Horses for riding, attended by a Coachman & Groom'. These are entries in his diary.

83 Overwork

17 years ago, a number of individuals, with myself, purchased the New Lanark establishment from the late Mr. Dale of Glasgow: at that period I found there were 500 children, who had been taken from poor-houses, chiefly in Edinburgh, and these children were generally from the age of 5 and 6, to 7 and 8; they were so taken because Mr. Dale could not, I learned afterwards, obtain them at a more advanced

period of life; if he did not take them at those ages, he could not obtain them at all. The hours of work at that time were 13, inclusive of meal times, and an hour and a half was allowed for meals. I very soon discovered that, although those children were extremely well fed, well clothed, well lodged, and very great care taken of them when out of the mills, their growth and their minds were materially injured by being employed at those ages within the cotton mills for $11\frac{1}{2}$ hours per day. It is true that those children, in consequence of being so well fed and clothed and lodged, looked fresh, and to a superficial observer, healthy in their countenances; yet their limbs were very generally deformed, their growth was stunted, and, although one of the best schoolmasters upon the old plan was engaged to instruct those children regularly every night, in general they made but a very slow progress, even in learning the common alphabet.

Select Committee on the state of children employed in manufactories 1816
English Historical Documents. Vol. XI

Glossary and notes
In many mills child workers suffered from long hours rather than actual cruelty. Robert Owen gave this evidence to a committee of M.P.s in 1816. He himself did not employ children under ten years of age.

84 Cruelty

Blincoe declared, that he had often been compelled, on a cold winter's day, to work naked, except his trousers, and loaded with two half hundredweights slung behind him, hanging one at each shoulder. Under this cruel torture, he soon sunk; when, to make the sport last the longer, WOODWARD substituted quarter of hundred-weights, and thus loaded, by every painful effort, Blincoe could not lift his arm to the roller. Woodward has forced him to wear these weights for hours together, and still to continue at his work!

For the sake of being the better able, and more effectually to torment their victims, the overlookers allowed their thumb and fore-finger nails to grow to an extreme length, in order that, when they pinched their ears they might make their nails meet, marks to be seen. Needham himself, the owner of the Mill, stands ARRAIGNED of having the cruelty to act thus, very frequently, till their blood ran down their necks, and so common was the sport, it was scarcely noticed.

Palfry, the Smith, had the task of rivetting irons upon any of the apprentices, whom the masters ordered, and those were much like the irons usually put upon felons. Even young women, if suspected of intending to run away, had irons rivetted on their ancles, and reaching by long links and rings up to the hips, and in these they were compelled to walk to and from the mill to work and to sleep. Blincoe asserts, he has known many girls served in this manner.

John Brown, 'A Memoir of Robert Blincoe', 1828

It was mainly in small remote mills that really bad cases of cruelty took place. Robert Blincoe, an apprentice at Litton Mill, in Derbyshire, described some instances to the man who was writing his life story. (See also p. 144.)

WOODWARD   an overlooker in the mill.

ARRAIGNED   accused.

From the statements and DEPOSITIONS obtained under the present inquiry in the several districts in England, and from all classes of witnesses, it appears that in the great majority of cases, corporal punishment is prohibited by the proprietors while it is proved on oath by several witnesses that operatives and overlookers have been suspended and even dismissed from their employment for disobeying this command. It is impossible to read the evidence from Leeds, Manchester, and the western district without being satisfied that a great improvement has taken place within the last few years in the treatment of children. What ill-treatment still exists is found chiefly in the small and obscure factories, while both in the large and small factories in England it is inflicted by workmen over children whom they themselves hire and pay, and who are completely under their control.

85 Improvement by 1833

Report of Commissioners on the employment of children in factories, 1833.
English Historical Documents, Vol. XII

Glossary and notes

By 1833 things seem to have improved, but notice the phrase *within the last few years*. The arrangement mentioned here, of children hired by the workmen, was quite usual. The mill-owner hired a man to take charge of a number of machines. The man then hired, and himself paid, several children as his assistants in the task.

DEPOSITIONS   written evidence given by witnesses.

The labour of lads in coal pits was excessive and its duration distressingly long . . . the poor boy was sent down below at the age of 6 to 8. If his parents were poor, and had a large family, he was sent early; his occupation was to open and shut a door to preserve the proper circulation of air, whilst the coals were passing from the workings to the shaft. He was called a trapper and had 5d a day; his labour is only light, but he must generally remain until the work is all done and the pit closed for the day. After going through this early stage of a pitman's life, he then becomes a driver or hurrier. The former attends a horse that draws coal in CORVES to a crane or the shaft; two of the latter take the coals from the workings themselves without the assistance of a horse. Here the misery of the latter begins, and generally continues until he is 17 or 18 years of age, when he is

86 Conditions in mines

considered fit to be a hewer. Previous to going down the pit, his education, when he had any, generally consisted of a little reading. . . . After he went to work, little time could be spared for education, unless for want of demand, the pits were not at full work.

Parliamentary Papers, Children's Employment Commission 1842, Appendix 1 pp. 675–6

Glossary and notes
The Report of the Commission on Children's Employment in 1842 gives a summary of the life of a miner from boyhood to adult life. A similar report (see extract 87, p. 80) is made on the use of young persons in the changing of blast furnaces.

Child labour was employed partly because it was cheap and also because a large family needed extra money to feed itself and no poor relief was allowed if there were children in the family who were able to work i.e. over six years of age.

CORVES   wooden tubs on rails for carrying coal.

87 Employment in ironworks

The boys are employed in filling coke into baskets or barrows and ironstone and limestone into boxes. . . . The young persons and the men convey these to the filling places at the top of the furnace. A certain proportion of each of the three is to be thrown into the furnace . . . from time to time. . . . There are generally two furnaces together and when the people have put the charge into the first furnace they go on to the next. There are never many minutes to rest but occasionally time may be got to snatch something to eat and drink. Thus they go on all day seven days a week until after four or five in the afternoon, and at that time the furnace is usually quite full. The boys and young persons then are allowed to go home and the blast is stopped for a time until the melted iron and cinder be let off.

First Report of Children's Employment Commission 1842, p. 48

The best little doorboy

88 The work of
youngsters in the
Rhondda mines

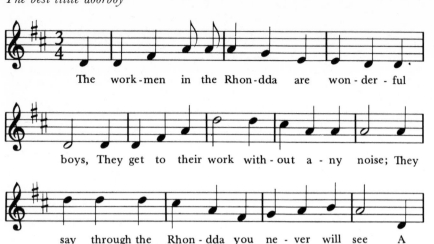

The work-men in the Rhon-dda are won-der-ful

boys, They get to their work with-out a-ny noise; They

say through the Rhon-dda you ne-ver will see A

merr-i-er lot than in Tip-per-ar-y. Too-ra-

loo,_____ too-ra-lay,_____ The

best lit-le door-boy that's un-der Jim Grey.

The workmen in the Rhondda are wonderful boys,
They get to their work without any noise;
They say through the Rhondda you never will see
A merrier lot than in TIPPERARY.

Chorus

Tooraloo, tooralay,
The best little DOORBOY that's under Jim Grey.

Old William, the lampman, and Dan with his horse,
And Daniel, the sawyer, is always so cross.
They say through the Rhondda you never will see
A merrier lot than in Tipperary.

Two girls from Treorchy pull out a full TRAM,
They've holes in their stockings, they don't care a damn
They say through the Rhondda you never will see
A merrier lot than in Tipperary.

O talk about hauling—it's nothing but fun,
To do her on the level as well as the run,
To hook her and sprag her and holler 'Gee-way!'
I'm the best little doorboy that's under Jim Grey.

Sung by Jack Randall;
collected by Alan Lomax
(Ewan MacColl, 'The Shuttle
and Cage', London edn.
1954, p. 25). The tune is
the well-known 'Villekins
and his Dinah'.

81

DOORBOYS   these boys were responsible for opening and closing the trapdoors which ensured that the ventilation system worked properly (see extract 86 p. 79).

TRAM   a wagon used to transport coal and pushed or pulled by women or children.

TIPPERARY   probably the name of a pit.

89 A different picture of work in a coalmine

The collier lass

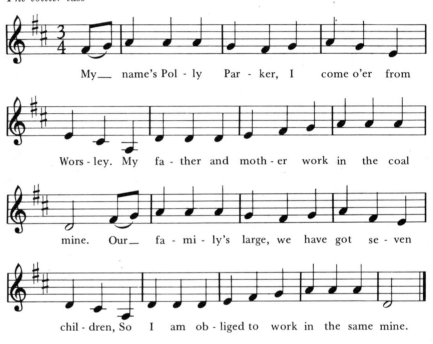

My name's Polly Parker, I come o'er from Worsley.
My father and mother work in the coal mine.
Our family's large, we have got seven children,
So I am obliged to work in the same mine.

And as this is my fortune, I know you feel sorry
That in such employment my days I shall pass,
But I keep up my spirits, I sing and look merry
Although I am but a poor collier lass.

By the greatest of dangers each day I'm surrounded.
I hang in the air like a rope or a chain.
The mine may fall in, I may be kill or wounded,
May perish by damp or the fire of the train.

And what would you do if it were not for our labour?
In wretched starvation your days you would pass,
While we could provide you with life's greatest blessing.
Then do not despise the poor collier lass.

All the day long you may say we are buried,
Deprived of the light and the warmth of the sun.
And often at nights from our bed we are hurried;
The water is in, and barefoot we run.

And though we go ragged and black are our faces,
As kind and as free as the best we'll be found,
And our hearts are as white as your lords in fine places.
Although we're poor colliers that work underground.

I am now growing up fast, somehow or other.
There's a collier lad strangely runs in my mind.
And in spite of the talking of father and mother,
I think I should marry if he was inclined.

But should he prove surly and will not befriend me,
Another and better chance may come to pass;
And my friends here I know, to him will recommend me,
And I'll be no longer a collier lass.

Broadside printed by Harkness, Preston (Madden Collection, Cambridge University Library). No tune specified. A Cheshire tune from a soul cakers' play is used here ('Journal of the English Folk Dance and Song Society', London, 1947, p. 90). Recorded by Frankie Armstrong ('Songs and Ballads', Topic 12TS273).

Glossary and notes

The ballad was probably printed about 1840 and is remarkable not only for its picture of coal-mining at that time but for its expression of the dignity of the *poor colliers that work underground.*

7
Labour
Relations

Providing for the workers

Labour relations between employers and employees varied not only from area to area, but also from mine to mine. Some employers like the Arkwrights, Robert Owen and Marquis of Rockingham were good employers and tried to deal fairly with employees. Others like the Clarkes and Blundells were poor employers and labour troubles often developed.

Tokens   Since there were few banks as we know them today, to overcome the shortage of cash, with which to pay wages, some employers minted their own trading tokens to act as a substitute. These were easily forged and mistrust of these as currency increased. Some employers paid their workmen partly in cash and partly in goods to overcome this defect in the supply of cash; this was known as the 'truck system'.

Tommy shops   Other employers developed the 'tommy shop'. These were shops owned by the employer at which the workmen could obtain goods on credit, so reducing the amount of ready cash needed for wages. The debts created at the 'tommy shop' were deducted from the wage packet of employees every week. No workman could leave his place of employment until his debts at the 'tommy shop' were cleared.

Complaints   It was customary to sign employment contracts on taking up employment. The coal owner claimed the right to fine his miners for sending coal mixed with dirt out of the mine. In the textile trade fines were collected for pieces badly woven and yarn badly spun. The transfer of industry from a hand or domestic one to a factory based one led to resistance and strikes. There was often friction between employer and workmen over differences in wage rates and standards of living.

90 Dealings with workers at Cromford

June 18
I saw the workers issue forth at 7 o'clock, a wonderful crowd of young people, made as familiar as eternal intercourse can make them; a new set then goes in for the night, for the mills never leave off working. Rocks, mills and water 'in confusion hurled'.

The stabling here is good; but poor Blacky, my new horse, has a bad cough, and begins today upon green meat, which we hope will cool his lungs. My walks of tonight were not extensive, for much is to be seen at hand: I soon return'd to tea; and, again early to supper.

The landlord has under his care a grand assortment of prizes, from Sr. R. Arkwright, to be given, at the year's end, to such bakers, butchers, &c, as shall have best furnish'd the market: how this will be peaceably settled I cannot tell!! They consist of beds, PRESSES, clocks, chairs, &c, and bespeak Sr. Rd's prudence and cunning; for without ready provisions, his COLONY cou'd not prosper: so the clocks will go very well. What the neighbouring market town of Wirksworth says to this, I have not heard.

Andrews, ed. 'The Torrington Diaries', 1954

Glossary and notes

PRESSES   cupboards.

COLONY   the early mills were usually in remote places, where water-power was available, but people were not. Here Cromford is called a *colony* and New Lanark a *new settlement* in no. 91, as if they were in other parts of the world. The early factory owners had to try to make their work attractive. Later, in the larger industrial towns workers were treated with less consideration.

Lord Torrington was staying at the Black Dog Inn in Cromford, in June 1790, when he made this entry in his diary. Notice Arkwright's way of making sure of good supplies of food etc. for his workers to buy.

91 Providing goods for the workers at New Lanark

New Lanark was a NEW SETTLEMENT formed by Mr. Dale; the part of the country in which these works were erected was very thinly inhabited; and the Scottish peasantry generally were disinclined to work in cotton mills; it was necessary that great efforts should therefore be made to collect a new population in such a situation, and such population was collected before the usual and customary means for conveniently supplying a population with food were formed; the workpeople were therefore obliged to buy their food and other articles at a very high price, and under many great disadvantages; to counterbalance this inconvenience, a store was opened at the establishment, into which provisions of the best quality, and clothes of the most useful kind, were introduced to be sold ... at a price sufficient to cover prime cost and charges, and to cover the accidents of such a business, it being understood ... that whatever profits arose from this establishment, those profits should be employed for the general benefit of the workpeople themselves; and these school establishments have been supported as well as other things, by the surplus profits.

Report of Committee on employment of children, 1816. Evidence of Robert Owen

Glossary and notes

NEW SETTLEMENT   see note on COLONY, *Glossary and notes* 90, p. 87.

ROBERT OWEN   the manager, and later the owner, of the New Lanark Mills.

92 The truck system

Messrs. Strutts of Belper in order to ensure a constant supply of Milk to the Inhabitants and make it the interest of Cow-keepers, to keep up their stock of Milking-Cows through the Winter, engage for a sufficiency of Milk, at $1\frac{1}{2}d$, $2d$, $2\frac{1}{2}d$, and even $3d$ per quart, during different periods of the year according to the expense and difficulties of procuring the article, and a person serves it out to their numerous

Workpeople in the Cotton Works, and keeps accounts until the end of the week, when they pay for it out of their wages.

J. Farey, 'A General View of the Agriculture and Minerals of Derbyshire', Vol. III, 1817

Glossary and notes

Strutts also obtained vegetables, meat, furniture, books and other goods for sale to their workers, who could pay for expensive items at so much per week, out of their wages. When the cost of rent and goods was deducted from the weekly wage it meant less actual coin was needed to pay the mill-hands.

93 A substitute for money

The tokens

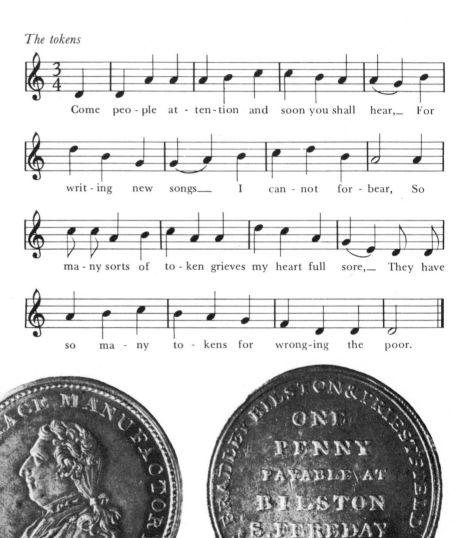

Come peo-ple at-ten-tion and soon you shall hear,— For writ-ing new songs— I can-not for-bear, So ma-ny sorts of to-ken grieves my heart full sore,— They have so ma-ny to-kens for wrong-ing the poor.

Token coins issued by Bradley of Bilston

Come people attention and soon you shall hear,
For writing of new songs I cannot forbear,
So many sorts of TOKENS grieves my heart full sore,
They have so many tokens for wronging the poor.

Here's tokens above, and here's tokens below,
And all sorts of tokens are made for to go.
Here's tokens of sorrow the world's full of evil,
And so many tokens will puzzle the Devil.

There's three shilling tokens are made for to pass,
There's tokens of silver and tokens of brass,
When I give you a token pray give it a ring,
Or else a bad token home soon you will bring.

Here's tokens of Forest's and tokens of Wood's
And tokens of Badger's; are Feredy's good?
For counterfeit tokens are sold by the score,
They are tokens of trouble to fall on the poor.

These tokens are made to support the town trade,
And thousands of tokens at Birmingham's made,
There's tokens of pleasures and tokens of fears,
If I told all the tokens I'd sing all the year.

What tokens they have the poor for to cross,
When they pass all the tokens, the poor bear the loss,
The token of charity's now got so small,
And the token of death will finish us all.

Broadside without imprint or title (Birmingham Reference Library, folder of
ballads no. 119932). No tune specified. 'Three pretty maidens' has been
used here (sung by William Hedge, Chipping Campden, Glos.; collected by
Cecil Sharp, 10 Aug. 1909, 'Journal of the Folk Song Society', London,
1914–16, vol. V, p. 64)

Glossary and notes

TOKENS   In the eighteenth century there was a serious shortage of copper and
small silver coins, and many employers used tokens of their own, which
would be accepted within a limited area. Most of them were made in
Birmingham. Of the manufacturers listed in the song, Forest of Lye, Wood
of Lye and Badger of Dudley all issued tokens in 1811 and Fereday of Bilston
in 1811–12. The three shilling tokens mentioned were issued by the Bank of
England in the early 1800s (Information supplied by Mr Anthony Gunstone
of the Birmingham City Museum and Art Gallery.)

The labour market

94 Finding work

A few Days since, between 40 and 50 North Britons, with Bagpipes and other Music playing, arrived at Cromford, near Matlock-Bath, from Perth, in Scotland. These industrious Fellows left that Place on account of the Scarcity of Work, were taken into the Service of Richard Arkwright, Esq. in his Cotton Mills and other extensive Works, entered into present Pay, and provided with good Quarters. They appeared highly pleased with the Reception they met with, and had a Dance in the Evening to congratulate each other on the Performance of so long a Journey.

'Derby Mercury' 1785

Glossary and notes

The idea that machines put men out of work is an old one. It is sometimes, but not always, true. In many places the building of factories provided work for people which they would not otherwise have had.

   This paragraph from the 'Derby Mercury' in 1785 reminds us that it might be necessary to travel far to find work. Long distance movement of people like this was rather unusual, however, although many Irish immigrants came in to Lancashire.

95 Shortage of labour at Elsecar, 1792

Dear Sir,

As colliers are now scarce and we are in want of them at Elsecar we must put ourselves to some inconvenience to procure them. John Lindley who many years ago wrought at Low wood is willing to leave Attercliffe where he now works and Engage at Elsecar provided we will accomodate him with a house and as the building in Stump Cross Lane has for some time been intended to be converted into two dwellings it seems to me the most advisable to do it as early as possible therefore I recommend that one end be immediately made into a House for John Lindley, who upon that assurance will give a month's notice to Quit his present employment, so that if you be of the same opinion must beg you will give direction for the alteration to be set about and that you will please to give John Lindley an answer according to the decision you make.—Michael Hague says that one man at present will be sufficient and he knows not where to find another.

I am in haste Dr. Sir,
Yours sincerely,
Charles Bowns
Sunday Morning May 27 1792.

Sheffield City Library, Wentworth Woodhouse Muniments, B.41.

Contracts and wages

Articles of agreement . . . between John Smith of Wilton Gilbert and . . . the several and respective workmen. In consideration of one shilling lawful money to them in hand paid for their binding money . . . they do hereby severally acknowledge and confess the receipt Also in further consideration of the rates and prices to be paid them . . . do hereby bind themselves to be his servants as hewers and fillers . . . And the said workmen do hereby severally promise and agree . . . that they will and well truly work for and abide with the said John Smith and no other person as his hewers and fillers . . . And the several workmen agree that the said John Smith shall keep and detain out of our wages one shilling for every day which we or any of us disturbeth the work or refuseth to work or insists on more wages than what is hereafter mentioned . . . And for every corve of coals that are deemed foul to pay one penny. And every person refusing to do so shall pay one shilling which the said John Smith shall keep and detain in his hand out of the wage or wages of persons so offending.

. . . And the said John Smith shall pay . . . once in every three weeks to the several workmen . . . thirteen pence a score for every score of coals . . . they shall hew . . . and fourpence a yard headways, and three pence a yard for walls . . . and allowing eight pecks of coals to each corve . . . and twenty one corves to the score.

T. S. Ashton & J. Sykes, 'The Coal Industry of the 18th century'. p. 242

96 A contract between owner and workers, 1767

Glossary and notes

Before the days of quick transport it was usual for a mine owner to depend entirely upon the supply of local labour for his mine. To keep a supply of labour and prevent a rival owner attracting a man away by offering higher wages, the owner would make the man sign a contract to work for him for a number of years. Sometimes the miner tried to use this contract to get higher wages and regular work. The Pitman's Bond of 1767 is an early type of contract. As you read this take note of what each workman is expected to do and the fine he must pay if he asks for more wages, disturbs the work or sends out tubs of coal below standard. Attached to this is a later type of agreement covering debts due to the Colliery for rent or goods from the 'tommy shop'.

26th March 1746 Between Samuel Walker of Grenoside in the parish of Ecclesfield ironfounder . . . and William Houlden of Southerhall in the same parish . . . Carpinter.

Samuel Walker hath by Request and desire of the said William Houlden consented . . . to take him into his Service to be imploy'd chiefly in the Ironfounder Business. But as Occasion may require in

97 Articles of Agreement for an ironfounder

the Carpinter Business to make new or Repair any thing the said Samuel Walker shall want for his own use for the Term of Ten Years . . . and to give him his wages weekly . . . for the first two years Seven Shillings . . . and for the two years after . . . Seven Shillings and Six pence and for the last Six Years Weekly . . . Eight Shillings . . . That William Houlden during the Term of Ten Years . . . shall not work either for himself or for any other person or persons than Samuel Walker . . . And that Samuel Walker . . . shall and will at the end of the first four Years of the said Term . . . give unto . . . William Houlden as much more Money weekly to be added to the eight shillings as will make his wages good and equal to any Servant . . . Samuel Walker shall employ. . . .

Sheffield City Library, Tibbets Collection TC.684

Glossary and notes

In the iron industry similar contracts were made for employment and a term of years was usually agreed upon.

98 Silkstone Colliery wages book

13th June 1833	Debts	Wages	Cash Paid	Balance
Isaac Armitage	5:6	£1:13: 0	£1: 7: 6	
Henry Holling	5:3	£1: 3: 4	£ 18: 1	
John Jones	13:3½	£2:18: 1½	£2:10:10	6:0
William Tordoff	11:3	£1:14: 2½	£1:11:11½	
Adam Hawksworth	7:4	£1: 1: 0	£ 13: 8	
George Hoyland	£8: 3:8	£2: 0: 3	£1: 6: 7	£7:10:0
Sam. Thompson	4:4½	£2: 5: 0	£2: 0: 7½	
Mary Naylor		7: 1	7: 1	
Martha Padgett		5:10	5:10	
George Holly	£3: 7:8½	£3: 9:11	£3: 6: 2½	£3: 4:0

Sheffield City Libraries, Clarke MSS. C.R.40

Glossary and notes

The extract from the wages ledger for 1833 shows how the Colliery owner recorded the debts and deducted a percentage from the man's wages each week, or if a small debt then the whole sum.

AGREEMENT
FOR STOPPAGES FROM WAGES.

Silkstone Colliery, near Barnsley, Yorkshire.

Articles of Agreement made and entered into by and between us, whose names are hereunto subscribed, being Artificers, Workmen, or Labourers of and for ROBERT COULDWELL CLARKE, of Silkstone Colliery, in the County of York, Coal Merchant, of the one part, and the said ROBERT COULDWELL CLARKE of the other part, as follows, that is to say :—

WE, whose names are hereunto subscribed, do hereby for ourselves, severally and respectively, contract and agree with the said Robert Couldwell Clarke, that he and his Agents shall and may, from time to time, stop, deduct, and retain out of our respective Wages, and the Wages of our Children, the Rent of any Tenements, with their Appurtenances, by him demised to, or occupied by us, respectively thereon reserved, or to be reserved. AND ALSO, all such Sum and Sums of Money as the said Robert Couldwell Clarke, or any of his Agents, shall or may advance or pay for us respectively, at our request, for or in respect of any Medicine or Medical Attendance. AND ALSO, the value of any Fuel supplied to us; or of any Materials, Tools, and Implements, to be by us respectively employed. AND ALSO, all such Sum and Sums of Money as the said Robert Couldwell Clarke, or any of his Agents, shall, at our request, advance to any of us, to be by us contributed to any Bank for Saving, or Friendly Society, (duly established according to Law,) or for Relief in Sickness, or for the Education of our Children, or any of them.

As Witness our Hands.

G. Harrison, Printer, Barnsley.

CR 135 H

Sheffield City Libraries, CR 135 H

Glossary and notes

Employees could buy goods on credit from the tommy shop, which was a store run by the colliery company. The cost would be deducted from their wages. The goods sold were often but not always of inferior quality.

Complaints by workers and owners

100 A complaint about fines for bad workmanship

Come all you cotton weavers

Come all you cotton-weavers, your looms you may pull down;
You must get employ'd in factories, in country or in town,
For our cotton masters have found out a wonderful new scheme,
These calico goods now wove by hand they're going to weave by steam.

In comes the gruff o'erlooker, or the master will attend;
It's 'You must find another shop, or quickly you must mend;
For such work as this will never do; so now I'll tell you plain,
We must have good pincopspinning, or we ne'er can weave by steam.'

There's sow-makers and dressers, and some are making warps;
These poor PINCOPSPINNERS, they must mind their flats and sharps,
For if an end slips under, as sometimes perchance it may,
They'll daub you down in black and white, and you've a shilling to pay.

In comes the surly winder, her COPS they are all marr'd;
'They are all snarls, and soft, bad ends; for I've roved off many a yard;

I'm sure I'll tell the master, or the joss, when he comes in':
They'll daub you down, and you must pay; – so money comes rolling in.

The weavers' turn will next come on, for they must not escape,
To enlarge the master's fortunes, they are fined in every shape.
For thin places, or bad edges, a GO, or else A FLOAT,
They'll daub you down, and you must pay, three pence, of else a GROAT.

If you go into a loom-shop, there's three or four pair of looms,
They are all standing empty, incumbrance of the rooms;
And if you ask the reason why, the old mother will tell you plain,
My daughters have forsaken them, and gone to weave by steam.

So, come all you cotton-weavers, you must rise up very soon,
For you must work in factories from morning until noon:
You mustn't walk in your garden for two or three hours a day,
For you must stand at their command and keep your shuttles in play.

Sung by John Grimshaw, Gorton, Lancs. (J. Harland, 'Ballads and songs of
Lancashire', London, 1865, p. 251, words only, under the title 'Hand-loom
v. power-loom'). No tune specified; a version of 'The bonny labouring boy'
has been used (sung by Thomas Hazelood, Ross. Herefs.; collected by
Cecil Sharp, 30 Aug. 1921, MSS. no. 4823).

Glossary and notes

Fines for bad workmanship were common. This song is a complaint about
them. The weavers are especially upset because they have been more used to
working on hand-looms, in their own homes. The first to go into the factories
were the women, to be followed by the men, who regretted the measure of
independence they had enjoyed as hand-loom weavers.

SOW   mixture of flour and water, used for sizing the warp (now called size).

COP   a small oval shaped bundle of spun cotton thread, prepared in that
form for the manufacture of cloth.

PINCOP   a regulation size cop ready for the shuttle.

FLOAT   a flaw in a piece of woven cloth caused by the shuttle passing over
the threads of the warp instead of between them.

WINDER   a person, usually a young woman, employed in a cotton factory to
wind weft on bobbins.

JOSS   an overlooker.

DRESSER   the worker who applies sizing to yarn or cloth.

GO   a piece of cloth which has to go back due to faulty workmanship.

GROAT   silver fourpenny piece.

The agents from the extensive collieries in the neighbourhood of
Wigan . . . came this evening with news of the colliers having left their
work and collected in a riotous manner to the number of near five
hundred . . . to demand an extravagant advance in wages. They have
given only til tomorrow at 3 o'clock to consider of it and if their
demand is not complied with, they threaten to destroy the Works

101 A request for troops to prevent a riot, October 1792

by pulling up the engines, throwing down the wheels and filling up the pits. The consequences ... would be serious ... if this consideration is not immediately suppressed. I am requested by the coal owners who are now with me to intreat of you to give orders to Major Campbell and the Commanding Officer at Manchester to march part of their men to Wigan in aid of the Magistrates. ...

Letter from Henry Blundell to Henry Dundas (Home Secretary for troops)

102 The coming of machines in the textile industry

The hand-loom weaver's lament

You gen - tle - men and trades - men, that ride a - bout at will, Look down on these poor peo-ple; it's e - nough to make you crill; Look down on these poor peo - ple, as you ride up and down, I think there is a God a - bove will bring your pride quite down.— You — ty - rants of Eng - land, your race will soon be run, You may be brought un - to ac - count for what you've sore-ly done.

You gentlemen and tradesmen, that ride about at will,
Look down on these poor people; it's enough to make you CRILL;
Look down on these poor people, as you ride up and down,
I think there is a God above will bring your pride quite down.

Chorus

You tyrants of England, your race will soon be run,
You may be brought unto account for what you've sorely done.

You pull down our wages, shamefully to tell;
You go into the markets, and say you cannot sell;
And when that we do ask you when these bad times will mend,
You quickly give in answer, 'When the wars are at an end'.

When we look on our poor children, it grieves our hearts full sore,
When clothing it is worn to rags, while we can get no more,
With little in their bellies, they to their work must go,
Whilst yours do dress as MANKY as monkeys in a show.

You go to church on Sundays, I'm sure it's nought but pride,
There can be no religion where humanity's thrown aside;
If there be a place in heaven, as there is in the Exchange,
Our poor souls must not come there; like lost sheep they must range.

With the choicest of strong dainties your tables overspread,
With good ale and strong brandy, to make your faces red;
You call'd a set of visitors—it is your whole delight—
And you lay your heads together to make our faces white.

You say that Bonyparty he's been the spoil of all,
And that we have got reason to pray for his downfall;
Now BONYPARTY'S DEAD and gone, and it is plainly shown
That we have bigger tyrants in Boneys of our own.

And now, my lads, for to conclude, it's time to make an end;
Let's see if we can form a plan that these bad times may mend;
Then give us our old prices, as we have had before,
And we can live in happiness, and rub off the old score.

Sung by John Grimshaw, Abbey Hey, Gorton, Lancs.; collected by J. Higson
(J. Harland, 'Ballads and songs of Lancashire', London, 1865, p. 259).
This ballad was sung to the favourite air of 'A hunting we will go'. The version
of the tune used here was sung (under the title 'A nutting we will go') by
Robert Hard, South Brent, Devon, and collected by H. F. Sheppard, 1889
(Baring-Gould MSS LXXXIII, Plymouth City Library). The song has been
recorded by Harry Boardman ('Deep Lancashire', Topic 12T 188).

Glossary and notes

Hand-loom weavers enjoyed a period of great prosperity in the 1780s, when
yarn was spun by machine but had to be woven by hand. After the invention
of the machine loom, however, wages for handloom weavers fell and they
became very badly-off. (See p. 98). The song tells of their hardship.

CRILL   goose-flesh.

MANKY   smart, immaculate.

BONAPARTY'S DEAD   the song dates from the years of depression after 1815.
Napoleon died in 1821.

Lancashire Record Office,

The handloom weavers in the Lancashire cotton industry had been very prosperous before 1800, as their skill was in demand to weave the greatly increased quantities of machine-spun yarn. After 1800 they were competing for work with the power loom, which was becoming more fool-proof and efficient. (See p. 14 on the dressing-frame.) They suffered also from disruption in the cotton trade brought about by the Wars with France, and the War of 1812 with the United States; and the high wartime cost of living.

This Petition was an attempt to get the J.P.s to fix wages, as they had the power to do, under Acts of Elizabeth I and James I. In fact the regulation of wages by J.P.s had fallen into disuse completely during the eighteenth century. Current laissez-faire thinking was totally against the revival of such a practice, and the Acts were in fact repealed that same year, 1813.

104 Other causes of poverty: the framework knitters

He found a female at work between nine and ten at night; her husband and two journeymen at work above her head up the step-ladder over the kitchen place she was occupying. Her age she stated to be fifty-three; she had the appearance of being seventy; there were bones, sinews, and skin, but no appearance of flesh. She had been the mother of fifteen children, ten of whom, male and female, her husband and herself had bred up to be stockingers. From sickness in a morning she could not work before her breakfast of tea, but laboured at night till ten o'clock, and her clear earnings were about 2s 6d weekly. She had worked the same frame nineteen years, and was making three feet at once to worsted hose. The frame had been 'patched up' twice in that time. The rent of it was 1s 6d a-week. The house rent was 2s 6d a-week. It was ill-drained, damp and unhealthy, as were all around it. She was however cheerful, uncomplaining, thankful, and even pious in her manner and speech.

Here was the female frame-work-knitter; the mother of other female stocking-makers, and of sons too—ten in all—added to the numbers of a trade grievously overloaded with labourers ever since they had belonged to it, and without prospect of relief. Her husband was a man of some character and standing, or he would not have been entrusted with four frames. He was one who made charges on his journeymen as well as paid them to the hosier; yet neither his labour, and the sum he received as a percentage on theirs, nor his poor wife's long hours and trifling earnings, nor, it seems, any other available means or motives, operated to send his children one after another into any better paid and more promising occupations. They seem to have had the idea that having come of a frame-work-knitting stock they must forever remain in that occupation.

W. Felkin, 'The History of Machine-Wrought Hosiery and Lace Manufactures', 1867

The framework knitters of the Midlands became one of the poorest classes of workers in the mid-nineteenth century. This was not because of competition from power-driven machines. Notice what the writer gives as the cause.

105 A cutler's attempt to reduce wages

Watkinson and his thirteens

That mon-ster op-pres-sion, be-hold how he stalks, Keeps
pick-ing the bones of the poor as he walks, There's
not a mech-an-ic through-out this whole land But what
more or less feels the weight of his hand;

That off-spring of ty-rann-y, base-ness and pride, Our
And may the odd knife his great car-case dis-sect, Lay

rights hath in-vad-ed and al-most des-troyed, May
o-pen his vi-tals for men to in-spect, A

that man be ban-ished who vil-lain-y screens: or
heart full as black as the in-fern-al gulph, In that

sides with big Wat-kin-son with his thir-teens.
gree-dy, blood-suck-ing and bone scra-ping wolf.

That monster oppression, behold how he stalks,
Keeps picking the bones of the poor as he walks,
There's not a mechanic throughout this whole land
But what more or less feels the weight of his hand;
That offspring of tyranny, baseness, and pride,
Our rights hath invaded and almost destroyed,
May that man be banished who villainy screens:
Or sides with big WATKINSON with his thirteens.

Chorus

And may the odd knife his great carcase dissect,
Lay open his vitals for men to inspect,
A heart full as black as the INFERNAL GULPH,
In the greedy, blood-sucking, and bone-scraping wolf.

This wicked dissenter, expelled his own church,
Is rendered the subject of public reproach:
Since reprobate marks on his forehead appear'd,
We all have concluded his conscience is sear'd:
See MAMMON his God, and oppression his aim,
Hark! how the streets ring with his infamous name,
The boys at the playhouse exhibit strange scenes
Respecting big Watkinson with his thirteens.

Like Pharaoh for baseness, that type of the de'il,
He wants to flog JOURNEYMEN with rods of steel,
And certainly would, had he got Pharaoh's power,
His heart is as hard, and his temper as sour;
But justice repulsed him and set us all free,
Like bond-slaves of old in the year jubilee.
May those be transported or sent for marines
That works for big Watkinson at his thirteens.

We claim as true Yorkshiremen leave to speak twice,
That no man should work for him at any price,
Since he has attempted our lives to ENTHRAL,
And mingle our liquor with wormwood and gall;
Come BEELZEBUB, take him with his ill-got PELF,
He's equally bad, if not worse than thyself;
So shall every cutler that honestly means
Cry 'take away Watkinson with his thirteens'.

But see foolish mortals! far worse then insane,
Three-fourths are returned into Egypt again;
Altho' Pharaoh's hands they had fairly escaped,
Now they must submit for their bones to be scraped;
Whilst they give themselves and their all for a prey
Let us be unanimous and jointly say,
Success to out Sovereign who peaceably reigns,
But down with both Watkinson's twelves and thirteens.

Written by Joseph MATHER
(J. Wilson, 'The songs of
Joseph Mather', Sheffield,
1862, p. 63). No tune specified. 'Packington's Pound', a
tune frequently employed for
satirical ballads in the seven-
teenth and eighteen centuries,
has been used here.

WATKINSON one of the principal manufacturers in the town, and master cutler in 1787. He died in 1790 or 1791.

MATHER (1738–1804) was a Radical balladeer very popular with the Sheffield working class. 'This (is) perhaps the most popular of Mather's songs . . . I can never forget the impression made on my mind when a boy on hearing it sung by an old cutler. This event happened on a "good saint Monday" [see *The jovial cutlers*], during a "foot ale" which was drank in the workshop. After the singer had "wet his whistle" he requested his shopmates to assist in chorus, and then struck off in a manly voice, laying strong emphasis on the last two lines in each stanza, at the conclusion of which he struck his stithy with a hammer for a signal, when all present joined in chorus with such a hearty good will that would have convinced any person that they felt the "odd knife" would have been well employed in dissecting Watkinson's "vile carcase". The popular opinion is that Watkinson was a "screw", and the first master who compelled his men to make thirteen for a dozen. It is further alleged that this song heart-broke him. This appears to have some support from the song "Watkinson's Repentance", one verse of which shows that the "god of the gallery" sang him out of the theatre.'

INFERNAL GULPH hell.

MAMMON wealth.

JOURNEYMEN qualified workers, who worked for an employer.

ENTHRAL enslave.

BEELZEBUB the devil.

PELF money.

106 Neglect of work

Joseph Banner of Belper, Nailer
Having been entrusted with a quantity of Iron to work up into nails and neglecting the performance of the same for the space of eight days.

Ordered by Mr Goodwin & Mr E. Strutt to work up the iron in six weeks & to pay the expenses (5/6d) in a fortnight.

Job Saunders of Duffield, Framework knitter
Wilfully neglecting for the space of eight days to work up certain cotton delivered to him to be worked into Stockings.

This was compromised by Job Saunders paying the expenses (4/-) and promising to finish the work in fourteen days.

Belper Petty Sessions Records

Glossary and notes
During the period of the Industrial Revolution, and up to 1867, whether in a factory or working at home, any worker who undertook to do a job was committing a crime if he did not do it. Cases like these were very common. These were heard at the Petty Sessions Court in Belper in the 1830s.

Letter from the miners to Jonathan Blundell

Nov. 20 1843

We the miners in your employ, beg leave most respectfully to call your attention to the present deplorable condition of ourselves and families, who we know by sad experience is mainly attributed to the very scanty pittance we receive as remuneration for our labours. . . . We do not remind you of the many dangers we have to incur when toiling in the bowels of the earth nor need we refer to the INSALUBRIOUS atmosphere we have to breathe or the unnatural position in which we have to labour . . . Our object in presenting you with this short address is to respectfully yet firmly demand a slight augmentation in the scale of prices, you are at present paying for the work we perform. In the name of that God who has declared, 'the labourer is worthy of his hire', we ask it on behalf of our once blooming but now hunger stricken and emaciated wives and children: we ask it on behalf of ourselves who . . . have to descend into the pit without breakfast for no other purpose but that you may be able to grow rich while we hunger and sink by slow degrees into a premature grave. . . .

The Miners in Your Employ
At the Wigan Cannel Works

Lancashire Record Office, Blundell Colliery MS.

Glossary and notes

INSALUBRIOUS   unhealthy.

I have been talking with a miner who tells me how as a child of seven years old he used to sit 12 or 13 hours a day behind his 'check door' at the pit bottom all alone and in the dark for his three shillings a week. I remember a poor little lad whom I passed every morning. I often found him crying and sobbing. I used to cut my candle in two and give him half of it. Long after that he was killed in the explosion at Oaks Colliery—he was only fifteen.

A boy begins his career as a lamp boy. He is the medium of communication between miners whose lamps have gone out or been rendered inefficient and the chief lamp man's room in the upper world. In process of time he rises to the dignity of a 'nipper'. The 'nipper' is an assistant to the horse driver. From 'nipper' to full blown horse driver is the natural move. The next step is the 'hurrier'. Hurrier is another name for loader, the man who fills the 'corves' that go in the trucks. Lastly comes the miner who wields the pick. The best men among the miners have their chance of becoming, sooner or later, under managers and deputies.

The 'ripper' not to be confused with 'nipper', clears off the roof to a height sufficient for the passages of horses with their loaded corves. He runs a fair chance of being buried alive. The deputy must be constantly on the watch for places that need propping up. It is no part of his duty to test the air in some stifling 'goaf', where naked men, in cramped attitudes, 'riddle' the 'slack' from the larger pieces of the fallen coal. . . .

The letter goes on to list the names of collieries where serious explosions have taken place.

Sheffield City Libraries, cuttings relating to Sheffield Vol. 11 p. 121

109 A pitman's wife on the subject of wages!

The coal-owner and the pitman's wife

A dia-logue I'll tell you as true as my life, Be-tween a coal-own-er and a poor pit-man's wife. As she was a-trav-'ling all on the high-way, She met a coal-own-er and this she did say, Der-ry down, down, down der-ry down.

A dialogue I'll tell you as true as my life,
Between a coal-owner and a poor pitman's wife.
As she was a-travelling all on the highway,
She met a coal-owner and this she did say,
Derry down, down, down derry down.

'Good morning, Lord Firedamp', this woman she said,
'I'll do you no harm, sir, so don't be afraid,
If you'd been where I've been the most of my life,
You wouldn't turn pale at a poor pitman's wife.'

'Then where do you come from?' the owner he cries.
'I come from hell', the poor woman replies.
'If you come from hell, then come tell me right plain,
How you contrived to get out again.'

'Aye, the way I got out, the truth I will tell.
They're turning the poor folk all out of hell.
This is to make room for the rich wicked race,
For there is a great number of them in that place.'

'And the coal-owners is the next on command
To arrive in hell, as I understand,
For I heard the old DEVIL say as I came out,
The coal-owners all had received their rout.'

'Then how does the old devil behave in that place?'
'Oh sir, he is cruel to the rich wicked race.
He is far more crueller than you can suppose,
Even like a mad bull with a ring through his nose.'

'If you be a coal-owner, sir, take my advice,
Agree with your men and give them a full price.
For if an you do not, I know very well,
You'll be in great danger of going to hell.'

Probably written by William Hornsby, a collier, of Shotton Moor, at the time of
the Durham Strike of 1844 (A. L. Lloyd, 'Come all ye bold miners', 1952,
p. 93). The 'Derry down' tunes were frequently used for songs of protest. The
song has been recorded by Ewan MacColl (Steam Whistle Ballads, Topic
12T 104).

Glossary and notes

DEVIL   the folk often looked on the devil as an ally rather than an adversary.

110 Report on West Riding collieries, 1842

Hunshelf Bank Webster and Peannes; a very small day pit, thin seam
with gates 24" to 30"; there are no horses and boys and girls hurry
together using belts and chains for hauling tubs.
Elsecar Earl Fitzwilliam; 80 foot shaft using round ropes and iron
conductors for winding; Seam 6 feet thick. It is an extensive colliery
with large wide gates; Few children employed and all males; Horses
are used and there is fire damp.
High Green George Chambers; Employ undertakers who contract for
getting coal from very thin seams. Horses used and there is fire damp.
Ironstone Thormcliffe Newton and Chambers; A day hole 9 feet high;
one large semicircular band face and one long horse gate.
Silkstone Mr Clarke; 90 foot shaft with flat ropes and iron conductors.
A six foot seam. A downcast shaft and a little gas. No girls employed
but horses used.
Barnsley Day and Ottibell; 198 feet deep shaft 1 foot six inch wide
ropes used and wooden conductors; 1 Ten foot thick seam; winding
wheels large and 2 corves drawn at once; large gates; no females; fire
damp.
Stainborough Copper; 100 foot shaft; using flat ropes and iron conductors.
Seam six feet thick horses used and some females employed; roof
shattered by gas.

Kexborough Wilson; 130 foot shaft; seam five feet six inches; Tackle similar to [Barnsley], no females employed but some fire damp.
Gawber George Thorpe; 80 foot shaft with flat ropes and iron conductors. The most regular large workings to be seen in Yorkshire; Corves 12 cwts when full; girls hurry with boys.
Mapplewell Wilson; 40 foot shaft worked by horse gin with round rope and chain; gates 1 yard high; a small pit with no females.
Flockton Henry Briggs; 1 shaft 60 feet and several 17 and 18 feet from horseway in upper seam; flat ropes with iron conductors; seams 15 inches to 16 inches thick. Internal shafts worked by hand windlass; gates only two feet and girls hurry with boys.

J. Goodchild Ms. Cusworth Hall, Doncaster

Glossary and notes
This Report on West Riding Collieries made in 1842 surveys all of the mines, but a few have been extracted which are situated in South Yorkshire. The equipment of each mine is described briefly and details of the labour employed. You will see that not all pits employed girls underground.

111 A boom period in the lace trade

Water or steam power had been applied several years to BOBBIN NET machinery in the larger establishments, between 1820 and 1822 it was much more so, and was the means of drawing machines into factories on all hands. Everything combined to lead the people in Nottingham and its neighbourhood, to expect golden times when the patent shackles were removed. In consequence, through the years 1823 to 1825, a time of unparalleled prosperity, capital flowed into the business abundantly from bankers, lawyers, physicians, clergymen, landowners, farmers, and retail dealers, in order to construct new lace machinery. That which was already at work could be sold for three times its cost. Every available smith and mechanic on the spot was hired, and the wonderful wages offered, speedily attracted smiths and mechanics from far off towns. Day labourers came from the plough and strikers from the forge, for some of the latter got £5 to £10 a-week. Birmingham, Manchester and Sheffield engineers and tool-makers met on one common ground; but houses were too few to lodge them; bricks doubled in price, and building land sold for £4000 an acre. Thousands of pounds were wasted in paying enormous weekly wages to people pretending to construct machinery, the movements of which they could not comprehend; and tens of thousands of pounds were drawn from speculators for machines, which, even if well constructed, could not possibly repay them their outlay. The inflation of the public mind was universal and became a sort of local epidemic—a mania, acquiring the name in after years of the 'twist net fever'. The whole community was athirst for gain, and became intoxicated. Nothing like it had ever been seen before in that trade or probably in any other. Those who actually wrought in the machines had an opportunity to realise large sums of money. The provident generally, as was natural, put their gains in a part, or the whole of a machine, paying for it by weekly instalments; thus becoming partly or wholly their own masters. The self-indulgent spent their time and money in a constant round of alternate work and pleasure. They would ride on horseback to and from labour, and having taken their shift at their machines, refresh themselves with a pint of port or claret at their return. Not a few of these spendthrifts were receiving parish pay or aid from public benevolence within the following ten years. The minds of many of the more ardent smiths and other mechanics became bewildered and overpowered, in the endeavour to overcome the difficulties presented by this intricate class of machinery, and they fell into insanity. When the speculative national frenzy of 1825, which had countenanced this more limited mania, collapsed in 1826, the effect in Nottingham and the district around was fearful. Visions of wealth and cherished schemes for grasping fortunes suddenly, were dissipated almost in a day. Many not in the trade, as well as some who were, lost all their means and fell into hopeless poverty; some died from despair; others went into self-imposed exile; a few destroyed themselves.

Nottingham Record Office

Glossary and notes

BOBBIN NET   a type of lace.

8
Recreations

'Sporting' times

Introduction

Sports, often of a brutal kind, had been the recreation of Englishmen for centuries. By 1760 many of these brutal sports had been discontinued but cock fighting, boxing (with bare fists) and horse racing were very popular. It should be remembered there was no half-day holiday on Saturday and the only holidays many people enjoyed were the great festivals of the Church. So sports took place on these days for there was no means of travelling far outside the locality in which people lived for entertainment.

The introduction of a Wakes week into the Lancashire Textile towns was an opportunity to lay on a programme of entertainment of all kinds such as public feast and firework displays. These survived as local recreations until the coming of the railways developed the seaside excursion. In those areas where domestic industry was strong it was the custom to do no work on Mondays.

Although poaching is often thought of as a 'sport', to many people it became as important as work. During the Napoleonic Wars and the depression that followed, food was very dear and many country people turned to poaching to provide their families with food. The landowners who had built up large estates were breeding game for the guests to shoot at house parties. Parliament passed the Game Laws which made poaching a penal offence and the punishment transportation.

Song, on a desperate Boxing Match, which was fought between Henry Griffiths, of Birmingham and Benjamin Baylis, of Wednesbury, near the town of Sutton, on Tuesday, October the 15th 1816.

A desperate boxing match

For staunch and firm bot-tom there ne-ver was known,_ A con-test more wor-thy of _ fame and re-nown,_ than one fought 'tween_ Grif-fiths and_ Bayles, _ of late,_ on_ con-quest both bent and for vic-t'ry e-late._

For staunch and firm BOTTOM there never was known
A contest more worthy of fame and renown,
Than one fought 'tween Griffiths and Baylis, of late,
On conquest both bent and for vict'ry elate.

October the fifteenth, at one in the day,
Began this most bloody and terrible fray;
Determin'd they both were, on ent'ring the field,
To forfeit their lives before ever they'd yield.

Two hundred and thirteen hard ROUNDS were display'd,
Not one nor the other e'er once seem'd afraid;
For more than four hours did the contest prevail,
And Vict'ry, o'er both, still held level her scale.

No shuffling, nor tricks, nor moment's delay,
Of cowardice once gave the smallest display;
For half-minute rests were all the rests giv'n,
To such severe fighting the contest was driv'n.

The seconds and umpires, unable to say,
On which side the contest the victory lay,
Declar'd a drawn battle, as th' only sure road,
To stop the two heroes from shedding more blood.

May Birmingham and Wednesb'ry henceforth agree,
And friends their inhabitants ever more be;
When they meet, be they social and quiet inclin'd,
And give their old grievances all to the wind.

Broadside in Birmingham Reference Library. Tune: 'Skewball'.

Glossary and notes

The years around 1800 were very 'sporting' times, sport then including cock-fighting, bull-baiting, etc. Boxing, with bare fists, was very popular both among the working class and some of the nobility. This song records in verse one famous fight.

BOTTOM   steadiness, grit.

ROUNDS   a round ended only when one of the fighters was knocked down. The contest ended when he was incapable of continuing.

113 Cock-fighting

The Cock-fight

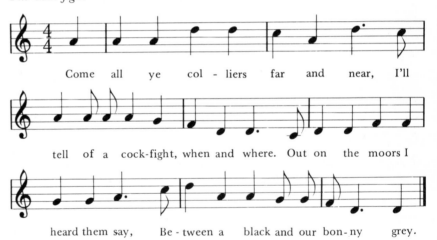

Come all ye col - liers far and near, I'll tell of a cock-fight, when and where. Out on the moors I heard them say, Be - tween a black and our bon - ny grey.

Come all ye colliers far and near,
I'll tell of a cock-fight, when and where.
Out on the moors I heard them say,
Between a black and our bonny grey.

First come in was the Oldham lads;
They come with all the money they had.
The reason why they all did say:
'The black's too big for the bonny grey'.

It's into the pub to take a sup,
The cock-fight it was soon made up.
For twenty pound these cocks will play,
The charcoal black and the bonny grey.

The Oldham lads stood shoutin' round:
'I'll lay ye a quid to half a crown,
If our black cock he gets fair play,
He'll make mincemeat of the bonny grey!'

So the cocks they at it, and the grey was tossed,
And the Oldham lads said: 'Bah, you've lost!'
Us collier lads we went right pale,
And wished we'd fought for a barrel of ale.

And the cocks they at it, one, two, three,
And the charcoal-black got struck in the eye.
They picked him up, but he would not play,
And the cock-fight went to our bonny grey.

With the silver breast and the silver wing,
He's fit to fight in front of the king,
Hip hooray, hooray, hooray!
Away we carried our bonny grey.

Lloyd, 'Come all ye bold miners', 1952, pp. 36/7.

Glossary and notes

Cock-fighting was popular until (and in some places after) it was made
illegal in 1849. Steel spurs were fitted to the spur of the cock and two birds
were matched in the cockpit with bets placed before the fight. The cock
which first killed its rival was the victor.

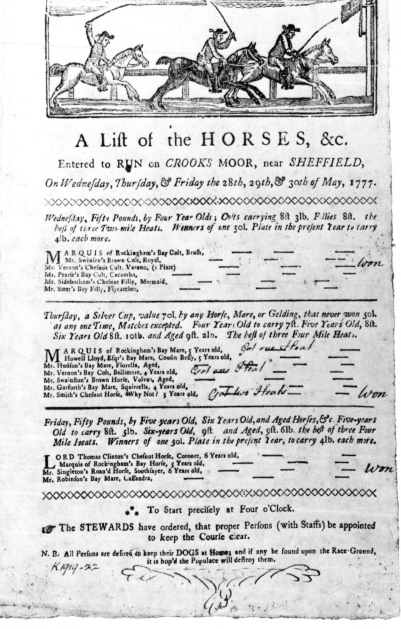

A List of the HORSES, &c.

Entered to RUN on *CROOKS* MOOR, near *SHEFFIELD*,

On *Wednesday, Thursday,* & *Friday the* 28*th,* 29*th,* & 30*th of May,* 1777.

Wednesday, Fifty Pounds, by Four Year Olds; Colts carrying 8ft. 3lb. *Fillies* 8ft. *the best of three Two-mile Heats. Winners of one* 50l. *Plate in the present Year to carry* 4lb. *each more.*

MARQUIS of Rockingham's Bay Colt, Brush,
  Mr. Swinfen's Brown Colt, Royal,
Mr. Vernon's Chesnut Colt, Varano, (1 Plate)
Mr. Pearse's Bay Colt, Cacambo,
Mr. Sidebotham's Chesnut Filly, Mermaid,
Mr. Steer's Bay Filly, Flycatcher, — — — Won

Thursday, a Silver Cup, value 70l. *by any Horse, Mare, or Gelding, that never won* 50l. *at any one Time, Matches excepted. Four Years Old to carry* 7ft. *Five Years Old,* 8ft. *Six Years Old* 8ft. 10lb. *and Aged* 9ft. 2lb. *The best of three Four Mile Heats.*

MARQUIS of Rockingham's Bay Mare, 5 Years old,   *Got one Heat*
  Howell Lloyd, Esqr's Bay Mare, Cousin Betty, 5 Years old,
Mr. Hudson's Bay Mare, Florella, Aged,   *Got one Heat*
Mr. Vernon's Bay Colt, Bellimore, 4 Years old,
Mr. Swainston's Brown Horse, Volvus, Aged,
Mr. Garforth's Bay Mare, Squirrella, 4 Years old,
Mr. Smith's Chesnut Horse, Why Not? 5 Years old,   *Got two Heats* — Won

Friday, Fifty Pounds, by Five-years Old, Six Years Old, and Aged Horses, &c. *Five-years Old to carry* 8ft. 5lb. *Six-years Old,* 9ft. *and Aged,* 9ft. 6lb. *the best of three Four Mile Heats. Winners of one* 50l. *Plate in the present Year, to carry* 4lb. *each more.*

LORD Thomas Clinton's Chesnut Horse, Coronet, 6 Years old,
  Marquis of Rockingham's Bay Horse, 5 Years old,
Mr. Singleton's Roan'd Horse, Soothsayer, 6 Years old,
Mr. Robinson's Bay Mare, Cassandra, — — — Won

*** To Start precisely at Four o'Clock.

☞ The STEWARDS have ordered, that proper Persons (with Staffs) be appointed to keep the Course clear.

N. B. All Persons are desired to keep their DOGS at Home; and if any be found upon the Race-Ground, it is hop'd the Populace will destroy them.

Sheffield City Museum

Glossary and notes

This horseracing bill for Sheffield 1777 shows how popular this sport was amongst South Yorkshire folks. Enclosure of the moor destroyed the racing at Sheffield in 1795.

Eccles Wake

Will be held on MONDAY and TUESDAY, the 30th, and 31st of August; and on WEDNESDAY and THURSDAY, the 1st, and 2d of SEPTEMBER, 1819.

On MONDAY, the ancient Sport of
BULL BAITING,
May be seen in all it's various Evolutions.
Same Day,
A DANDY RACE,
For a PURSE of SILVER—the best of heats—The second-best to be entitled to 5s.
Same Day,
A FOOT-RACE for a HAT,
By Lads not exceeding Sixteen years of age.—Three to start, or no race.
On TUESDAY,
A JACK-ASS RACE,
For a PURSE of GOLD, value £50.—The best of three heats,—Each to carry a feather.—The Racers to be shewn in the Bull-ring exactly at 12 o'clock, and to start at 2.—Nothing to be paid for entrance : but the bringer of each Steed to have a good Dinner gratis, and a quart of strong Ale, *to moisten his clay.*

Same Day,
A FOOT-RACE for a HAT,
By Lads that never won a Hat or Prize before Monday.—Three to start.
Same Day,
An APPLE DUMPLING Eating,
By Ladies and Gentlemen of all ages: The person who finishes the repast first, to have 5s.—the second, 2s.—and the third, 1s.
On WEDNESDAY,
A PONY RACE,
By Tits not exceeding 12 hands high, for a CUP, value £50.—The best of heats.—Three to start, or no race.
Same Day,
A Foot-Race for a Hat, value 10s. 6d.
By Men of any description.—Three to start.
Same Day,
A Race for a good Holland Smock,
By *Ladies* of all ages: the second-best to have a handsome Satin Riband. Three to start.
On THURSDAY,
A GAME AT PRISON-BARS.
Also,
A GRINNING MATCH through a Collar.
For a Piece of fat Bacon.——No *Crabs* to be used on the occasion.
Same Day,
A YOUNG PIG
Will be turned out, with his Ears and Tail well *soaped,* and the first Person catching and holding him by either, will be entitled to the same.
Smoking Matches, by Ladies and Gentlemen of all ages.
To conclude with a grand FIDDLING MATCH, by all the Fiddlers that attend the Wake, for a Purse of Silver.—There will be prizes for the second and third-best—Tunes ; "O where, and O where does my little Boney dwell. Britons strike home—Rule Britannia—God save the King." May the King live for ever, huzza!

N.B. As TWO BULLS in great practice are purchased for diversion, the Public may rest assured of being well entertained. The hours of Baiting the Bull, will be precisely at 10 o'clock in the Morning for practice, and at 3 and 7 o'clock for a prize. The dog that does not run for practice is not to run for a prize.
The Bull-ring will be stumped and railed all round with Oak Trees, so that Ladies or Gentlemen may be accommodated with seeing, without the least danger.—Ordinaries, &c. as usual.
☞ The Bellman will go round a quarter of an hour before the time of Baiting.

GOD SAVE THE KING.

JOHN MOSS, Esq ⎱ STEWARDS.
T. SEDDON, Esq ⎰
T. CARRUTHERS, Clerk of the Course.

J. Patrick, Printer, Manchester.

Manchester Public Libraries

Glossary and notes

Wakes weeks in Midland and Northern towns meant the traditional annual holiday (unpaid, of course). During its Wakes, the town would be visited by many kinds of performers, jugglers, card-tricksters, and so on. Shows like those described in the advertisement were also put on.

Remember that the apple dumplings on Tuesday would be steaming hot. The idea of a grinning match was to see which boy could pull the best, or worst, face. The horse-collar acted as a frame for the picture!

116 A colliers' feast at Elsecar

March 6th 1769   paid for Colliers feast

Malt and Hops	1 : 4½d
Beef	14 : 3d
Veal	3 : 1d
Bread	1 : 2d
Butter	1 : 4d
Tobacco and Pipes	11d

£1 : 2 : 1½

Sheffield City Libraries, Wentworth Woodhouse Muniments. A 1585

Glossary and notes

Little is known about these colliers' feasts but from the records in the Wentworth Woodhouse archives, they appear to have been annual events in which beer and a huge meal played a prominent part.

117 A firework display

STORMING of ST. JEAN D'ACRE, &c.
AT THE
BOTANICAL GARDENS.

The Inhabitants of Sheffield, Rotherham, and the neighbourhood, are respectfully informed, that the UNRIVALLED PYROTECHNIST,

MR. BYWATER,

Has undertaken to exhibit,

On MONDAY NEXT,

The 20th of September instant, A DISPLAY OF

FIREWORKS,

OF NOVEL & EXTRAORDINARY CHARACTER.

When, amongst other new and beautiful Devices, he will introduce the

ROYAL VICTORIA PIECE,

As exhibited by him before the Queen, by special appointment, and of which her Majesty was pleased to express her high admiration.——Likewise, his

MAGNIFICENT FOUNTAIN PIECE,

Giving a VIEW of the CELEBRATED WATERWORKS in CHATSWORTH PARK.

To conclude with a

New and Imposing MILITARY SPECTACLE,

REPRESENTING THE

STORMING

OF

ST JEAN D'ACRE,

BY COMMODORE NAPIER.

With a View of that city, (painted on upwards of 100 feet of canvas,) which, after a prolonged cannonade, will be involved in an OVERWHELMING CONFLAGRATION, and terminate with a TERRIFIC EXPLOSION of the MAGAZINE ; the entire Piece forming a rare and unique combination of Panoramic and Pyrotechnic Display.

Sheffield City Libraries

This advertisement for a firework display in 1840 in the Botanical Gardens,
Sheffield, will help you to understand how magnificent these were and on
what a large scale they were carried out.

The jovial cutlers

118 A nagging wife

Bro - ther work - men, cease your la - bour,

Lay— your files and ham - mers by; Lis - ten while a

bro - ther neigh - bour sings— a cut - ler's des - tin - y.

How up - on a good Saint Mon - day,

Sit - ting by— the smi - thy fire, Tell - ing what's been

done o't Sun - day, And— in cheer - ful mirth con - spire.

Brother workmen, cease your labour,
Lay your files and hammers by;
Listen while a brother neighbour
Sings a cutler's destiny—
How upon a good SAINT MONDAY,
Sitting by the smithy fire,
Telling what's been done o't Sunday,
And in cheerful mirth conspire.

Soon I hear the trap-door rise up,
On the ladder stands my wife:
'Damn thee, Jack, I'll dust thy eyes up,
Thou leads a plaguey drunken life;
Here thou sits instead of working,
Wi' thy pitcher on thy knee;
Curse thee, thou'd be always lurking,
And I may slave myself for thee.'

Now her passion sets her tongue fast,
Rage won't give her malice sway;
And her clapper, which did ring fast,
For want of breath is forced to stay;
Her eyes boil up with fire and fury,
Anger makes her cheek look pale;
And her power to let the men see,
Again her voice our ears assail:

'Ah! thou great, fat idle devil,
Now I see thy goings on;
Here thou sits all 't day to revel,
Ne'er a stroke o' wark thou's done;
If thou canst but get thy tankard
Thou neither thinks o'wark nor me:
Curse thee, I was sorely hampered
When I married a rogue like thee.'

All you who, blinded by delusion,
Matrimony never knew,
Cannot judge of my confusion,
But may think my tale untrue,
For her foul tongue it's past bearing,
Her looks are full of foul disdain;
Ranting, railing, tearing, swearing,
Hark! her clapper rings again.

'See thee, look what stays I've gotten,
See thee, what a pair o' shoes;
Gown and petticoat half rotten,
Ne'er a whole stitch in my hose,
Whilst broiled up with noise and racket,
Thou'd'st swallow more than would fill a butt—
Damn it, tak' it—devil tak' it,
It's better there than in thy gut.'

Now she speaks with motion quicker
Than my boring stick at Friday's pace;
She throws the generous sparkling liquor
With all her fury in my face;
My eyes, my apron, and my breeches,
My poor shirt sleeves are drench'd with ale.

Something bad my dear bewitches,
Again to vex us with her tale.

'Pray thee, look here, all the forenoon
Thou's wasted with thy idle way;
When does t'a mean to get thy SOURS done?
Thy mester wants 'em in today;
Thou knows, I hate to broil and quarrel,
But I've neither soap nor tea;
Od burn thee, Jack, forsake thy barrel,
Or never more thou'st lie wi' me.'

Now once more on joys be thinking,
Since hard scolding's tired my wife;
The course is clear, let's have some drink in,
And toast a jovial cutler's life;
For her foul tongue, Oh! fie upon her,
Shall we our pleasures thus give o'er?
No! we will good Saint Monday honour,
When brawling wives shall be no more.

'Miscellaneous songs relating to Sheffield' (appendix to 'The
Songs of Joseph Mather', Sheffield, 1862), p. 88, to the tune of 'Cease,
rude Boreas'. The version of the tune used here was sung by Mr Gibbs,
Evesham, Worcs., and collected by Cecil Sharp, 7 Apr. 1909 (Sharp MSS. no. 2128).

Glossary and notes

SAINT MONDAY   the text of this song dates from the late eighteenth century
and refers to the practice, widespread then and for many years afterwards
among workers particularly in certain trades, of doing no work on Mondays
('keeping Saint Monday').

SOURS   pieces of work paid for, but not completed.

Poachers

NOTICE IS HEREBY GIVEN,
THAT STEEL TRAPS and SPRING GUNS are
constantly set in all the Woods and Plantations of
EDWARD MILLER MUNDY, Esq within the several Townships
or Liberties of Shipley, Heanor, Mapperley, and Smalley, in
the County of Derby.
Shipley, Oct. 1st, 1817.

119 Steel traps and
spring guns

Derby Central Library, 'Derbyshire Chronicle', 1 October 1817

Glossary and notes

Poaching might be thought of as an occasional means of getting some food for
oneself; it might be a more or less regular way of making a living; or it could
be done as a very risky but exciting and perhaps profitable form of recreation.
Notices like the following made poaching on some lands a very deadly sort of
sport, but some people would still risk it.

120 A warning against poaching

Henry's downfall

Come all you wild and wicked youths, wher-ev-er__ you may__ be, I pray you give at-ten-tion and__ lis-ten un-to me; The fate of us poor__ trans-ports, as__ you shall un-der-stand, The hard-ships that we un-der-go up-on Van__ Die - - man's__ land.

Come all you wild and wicked youths, wherever you may be,
I pray you give attention and listen unto me;
The fate of us poor transports, as you shall understand,
The hardships that we undergo, upon VAN DIEMAN'S LAND.

Chorus

Young men all now beware,
Lest you are drawn into a snare.

My parents reared me tenderly, good learning gave to me,
Till with bad company I was beguiled, which proved my destiny
I was brought up in Lancashire, near Bolton town did dwell,
My name it is young Henry, in Chorley known full well.

I and five more went out one night, into a squire's park,
Hoping we could get some game, the night it proved dark,
But to our great misfortune, they TREPANNED us with speed,
And sent us to Lancaster, which made our hearts to bleed.

It was at the March Assizes to the bar we did repair,
Like Job we stood with patience to hear our sentence there,
There being some old offenders, which made our case go hard,
My sentence was for 14 YEARS, I was quickly sent on board.

The ship that bore us from the land, the Speedwell was its name
For full five months and upwards, boys, we ploughed the raging main,
Neither land nor harbour could we see, believe it is no lie,
All around us one black-water, boys, above us one blue-sky.

I often looked behind me towards my native shore,
That cottage of contentment, that I never shall see more,
Nor yet my own dear father, who tore his hoary hair,
Likewise my tender mother, the woman that did me bear.

On the fifteenth of September, then we soon did make the land
At four o'clock we went on shore, all chained hand-to-hand,
To see our fellow sufferers, we felt I can't tell how,
Some chained to a harrow, and others to a plough.

No shoes or stockings they had on, nor hat had they to wear,
But a HURDEN frock and LINSEY drawers—their feet and head were bare;
They chained them up by two-and-two, like horses in a team,
Their driver he stood over them with his Malacca cane.

Then I was marched to Sidney Town, without any more delay,
Where a gentleman he bought me, his book keeper to be,
I took his occupation—my master liked me well,
My joys were out of measure, I'm sure no tongue can tell.

We had a female servant, Roseanna was her name,
For fourteen years a convict was, from Liverpool she came,
We often told our tales of love, when we were blest at home,
But now we're rattling of our chains, in foreign lands to mourn.

Broadside printed by J. Russell, Moor Street, Birmingham (British Museum 1876 e 2). Tune: sung by Mr Anderson, King's Lynn, Norfolk; collected by R. V. Williams, 9 Jan. 1904 ('Journal of the Folk Song Society', vol. II, p. 166). A similar song has been recorded by John Faulkner ('Waterloo-Peterloo', Argo DA 68), under the title of 'Van Dieman's Land'

Glossary and notes

Popular songs about poaching sometimes treated it in a spirit of bravado and gaiety—like pot-holing, rock-climbing, or car-racing of the present day. Other songs, like 'Henry's downfall' were intended to warn young men of the dangers involved.

Eighteenth- and nineteenth-century folk songs like this one were often known as 'come-all-ye's', from the opening words. They were intended to be sung in public places and the first line or even the first verse did not begin the story itself. It gave people a little time to gather round the singer. The third and fourth lines of the second verse can easily be altered to include almost any county and town. The chorus may be omitted, spoken, or sung to the tune of the last line.

VAN DIEMAN'S LAND Tasmania—poachers were transported to New South Wales and Tasmania from 1800 onwards.

TREPANNED trapped.

FOURTEEN YEARS the sentence of fourteen years' transportation (when three men, one of whom carried a gun or bludgeon were found in a wood) was brought in by an Act of 1828. Long after transportation ceased, its brutality remained imprinted on people's imagination.

HURDEN a rough cloth.

LINSEY a wool and cotton cloth.

Gardens

121 The popularity of horticulture

. . . Fifteen or twenty years ago the most barbarous kinds of sports were practised by the men such as bull baiting, dog fighting, cock fighting etc. These have gradually died away and are now practised upon a very limited scale. . . . This is caused by the education of the rising generation.

Their mode of spending their leisure hours differs very much; most of them have gardens, and many of them take great delight in the cultivation of flowers and have, 'flower shows' during the season. In winter they have no mode of employing their vacant time, and they spend it unprofitably; this may be accounted for from the small numbers of them who can read. . . .

Benefit Societies are established in almost every village . . . from which members receive weekly sums when they are ill or have an accident; and also a sum when any member or his wife dies. These societies have been of infinite service and have been the means of preventing many families from applying for parish relief. There are other benefit societies, now established attached to associations of 'Odd Fellows', 'Foresters' etc which have had an excellent effect not only in helping each other in distress but by promoting a more temperate course of life. . . .

Parliamentary Papers, Children's Employment Commission 1842
App. Pt 1 p. 718

Glossary and notes

This extract describes the popularity of horticulture, a hobby which is still very common in mining communities and many miners take pride in their skill in growing flowers for flower shows. You will also read about the benefits the Friendly Societies brought to these communities.

122 The gift of a park

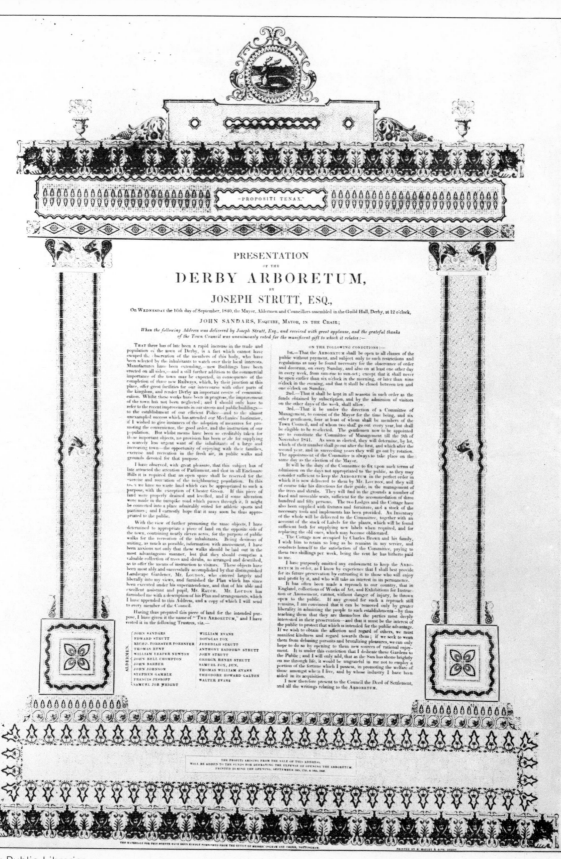

When towns grew, many people could no longer easily reach the countryside. This document—a souvenir of the occasion—is about this. Notice that admission is free only on Sunday and at least one other day. Notice also the kindly view of the common people which Joseph shows in the last paragraph. *Propositi Tenax* is the Latin motto of the Strutt family. It means 'Tenacious in Purpose'.

9
Combinations,
Self Help
and Education

Introduction

The years 1793–1815 were the years of war with France. During and after the war, the government, which represented the upper classes, clamped down hard on any sign of unrest among the people.

The Combination Acts of 1799 and 1800 had forbidden the combining of working men into unions or 'combinations' for the purpose of obtaining increased wages and better working conditions. But these unions continued to exist and were a source of concern to the authorities for they feared the outbreak of a revolution like the one in France in 1789. It was not until the 1820s that their fear of a revolution of the 'lower orders' began to fade.

Improvements in wages and working conditions which were obtained by a union helped all the members equally. There were also a number of ideas, known as 'self help', aimed at helping a worker to educate and improve himself so that he, as an individual, could get a more responsible and better-paid job. Attempts were also made at improving the morals of the workers: in the nineteenth century this usually meant getting people to stop drinking too much beer, gin etc. The Temperance Societies aimed to do this.

Combinations

123 Methods used in Sheffield to spread the ideas of Tom Paine and others

Hertford Street   13th June 1792

The mode they have adopted for spreading their LICENTIOUS principles has been by forming Associations on terms suited to the circumstances of the lowest mechanics of whom about 2,500 are enrolled in the principal society and that it may not be confined, they allow any man to be present who will pay 6d for admission. Here they read the most violent publications, and comment on them, as well as on their correspondence not only with the dependent Societies in the town and villages in the vicinity but with those established in other parts of the kingdom. . . .

Letter from Colonel de Lancey to the Secretary of State; Sheffield City Libraries

Glossary and notes
LICENTIOUS   dissolute, uncontrolled.

124 Growth of combinations, and strikes for higher wages

Makeney, near Derby
14 March 1814

I presume to call the attention of your Lordship to a subject which, if not timely checked, will at a future period render all your efforts to do so fruitless, and will eventually destroy our superiority over other countries in manufacture. What I allude to is the combination of workmen to demand an increased price for labour, or what the manufacturers term 'striking'. This is now taking place to a considerable extent in our principal towns and will spread to all if not prevented. . . .

Sheffield City Library, Wentworth Woodhouse Muniments

1814 Advances of wages, immoderate beyond all means, have been demanded by the men and means equally violent and illegal employed to enforce them. The evil . . . has now made progress so alarming as to threaten the most dangerous consequences to the trade. . . .

1819 The workmen's deputies [are concerned] by the extraordinary depressed state to which the trade of the town is reduced . . . a remedy must be found for what might otherwise reduce to a mass of ruin and pauperism every respectable manufacturer and workman in this once happy and flourishing neighbourhood.

The deputies appointed by the workmen earnestly request the master manufacturers to meet them to consult on the best means to be adopted to check these evils[1]—a very significant attempt to achieve that co-operation between capital and labour which is still more frequently talked about than attained.

Sheffield City Libraries, cuttings relating to Sheffield Vol. 10

125 Press reports on the effect of strikes on Sheffield prosperity

The author served for a whole year (at this time of alarm) as a special constable, and though so young had others, at first civilians and afterwards foot soldiers to lead every second or third night. In the latter case six men armed with muskets were TOLD OFF, and at 5 p.m. having received the instructions and pass-word from the sitting magistrate, he did the duty of patrolling with them in the town until six the following morning. The responsibility was new and weighty, and not altogether unattended with danger, the LUDDITES being armed; and knowing they hazarded their own lives, they were not chary of the lives of others. Their daring and courage were shown in the instance of one who entered a house alone in Rutland Street, Nottingham, one evening; proceeded up stairs and smashed the material parts of a frame in a minute or two; but that short time was sufficient to cause an alarm; constables were in front of the house, and the author happened to be on duty, in Park Street, behind it. The man at once perceived his danger, threw himself on the roof; passing along others he saw in the dim light that the earth had been lately turned up in a garden below, and leaped from the eaves of a three-story house upon it. The frame-breaker quietly passed through a kitchen where a family were at table, and escaped. In a few minutes the shouts of a sympathising crowd were heard at New Radford, half-a-mile from the scene of the adventure.

W. Felkin, 'The History of the Machine-Wrought Hosiery and Lace Manufactures', 1867

126 A Luddite incident

[1] Cut throat competition.

The writer, Felkin who was 17 at the time, describes a small incident which occurred in Nottingham during the winter of 1811–12.

TOLD OFF   appointed for duty.

LUDDITES   men who went around smashing machinery (in this case stocking frames), as a way of protesting about unemployment, low wages, and the strict attitude of the authorities.

127 Luddites destroy shear frames

The croppers' song

Come cropper lads of high renown,
Who love to drink good ale that's brown
And strike each haughty tyrant down
With hatchet, pike and gun.

Chorus

Oh, the cropper lads for me,
The gallant lads for me,
Who with lusty stroke the shear frames broke,
The cropper lads for me.

Who though the SPECIALS still advance
And soldiers nightly round us prance,
The cropper lads still lead the dance
With hatchet, pike and gun.

And night by night when all is still
And the moon is hid behind the hill,
We forward march to do our will
With hatchet, pike and gun.

Great ENOCH still shall lead the VAN.
Stop him who dare, stop him who can.
Press forward every gallant man
With hatchet, pike and gun.

F. Peel, 'The Risings of the Luddites', Heckmondwike, 1888, p. 46. A. L. Lloyd fitted a traditional tune to the words. Recorded by Roy Harris ('Champions of folly', Topic 12TS256)

Glossary and notes

In the early 19th century, shearmen or croppers, who trimmed the nap of cloth with huge shears, were being made redundant by the use of machines for finishing woollen cloth. Gangs of them went about smashing the shear-frames as the Midlands Luddites broke stocking-frames, and Lancashire men attacked power-loom mills.

SPECIALS   special constables, like Felkin in Nottingham.

VAN   the 'vanguard' or advance party, who lead the attack.

ENOCH   the name for the sledge-hammer which they carried. It was named after Enoch Taylor, a partner in the firm which also built the shearing frames.

128 How some people still thought of Trade Unions in 1834

Radio Times Hulton Picture Library

TO THE

Gentry and other Inhabitants

OF

BELPER,

AND THE NEIGHBOURHOOD.

It has been deemed advisable to make this appeal to you, on behalf of our **TRADES' UNION**; knowing, and hearing so frequently, that some of our Employers, and other enemies, have given false and malicious representations of our Society. Be it remembered, that our Society is for the purpose of promoting general and useful knowledge, improving the morals of its Members, encouraging peace, harmony, and brotherly love, and cultivating a good understanding amongst each other; and to consider that the whole depends upon these laws being abided by. And that every Member who breaks the laws of the land, either by embezzleing his master's property, theft, highway robbery, or any other felony or crime, cognizable by the law; or who shall, either publicly or privately, assault or injure any individual, either by breaking their windows, or otherwise destroying their property, shall be considered the greatest enemy to, and be expelled from, never more to enter, our Society. We hope this will sufficiently satisfy the respectable inhabitants of **BELPER**, and its neighbourhood, that our meaning is to "*do unto others as we would that they should do unto us.*"

Should any further information be required, it will be given, by applying at any of the Lodges.

N.B. No Disloyal Toasts are given, or Political Subjects discussed, at any of our Meetings.

BELPER, December 2, 1833.

G. JEWITT, PRINTER, DUFFIELD.

Derby Borough Libraries

Glossary and notes

Even nine years after Trade Unions had been made legal in 1824, the members felt it necessary to assure *the gentry and other inhabitants* that they were not a dangerous society of criminals. The fashion in 1833 was to have a local union of all trades instead of a national Union for each separate trade, as nowadays, like the N.U.R., or the N.U.T.

ENGLISHMEN!

THE few remaining liberties which a Tyrannical Oligarchy has left to the Enslaved People, have been this day forcibly taken from You in Birmingham by an Armed Power.

In vain does the British Constitution declare that every Subject has a right to petition the Queen on his Grievances. The Government, through the Magistrates, have denied that right; and have, in opposition to every principle of Justice, and of the Constitution, prevented a Meeting, called for the purpose of Peaceably Memorializing the Queen: having first brought into the Town an ARMED POWER to enforce their unjustifiable and unconstitutional Proceedings.

We issue out our

Solemn Protest

against such undisguised Tyranny; declaring, that, if such an encroachment on the Rights of Englishmen is submitted to, there will be no longer Freedom for any class. Tyranny preserving its power only by abridging the Liberties of all.

We record it as our deliberate opinion, that the Ruling Power has taken away the just and Constitutional Rights of the People, and that circumstances have now arisen, in which the Government has no rightful claim to our allegiance.

PASSIVE RESISTANCE on our part is not only a Right but a SACRED DUTY.

WE RESOLVE

NOT TO OBEY THE GOVERNMENT

BY SERVING THEM IN ANY CAPACITY.

WE RESOLVE NOT TO RECOGNIZE THEM AS OUR GOVERNMENT; We, therefore, REFUSE

TO PAY ALL TAXES.

Signed, by order of the Committee,

Christian Chartist Church.   ARTHUR O'NEILL, Secretary.

Trueman, Printer, Chartist Press, Newhall-street, Birmingham.

130 A Chartist notice calling on Englishmen to withhold taxes

Lambeth Palace Library

HYMN,

BY EBENEZER ELLIOTT.

Written specially to be Sung at the

MEETING OF THE WORKING CLASSES,

TO BE HELD

AT SHEFFIELD, SEPT. 25, 1838.

———

TUNE—*The Old Hundred Psalm.*

———

GOD of the Poor! shall labour eat?
Or drones alone find labour sweet?
Lo, they who call thy earth their own,
Take all we have—and give a stone!

Yet bring not Thou on them the doom
That scourged the proud of wretched Rome,
Who stole, for few, the lands of all,
To make all life a funeral.

Lord! not for vengeance rave the wrong'd,
The hopes deferr'd, the woes prolong'd,
Our cause is just, our Judge divine;
But judgment, God of all, is thine!

Yet not in vain thy children call
On Thee, if Thou art Lord of all;
And by thy work, and by thy word,
Hark! millions cry for justice, Lord!

For leave to toil, and not in vain—
For honest labour's needful gain;
A little rest, a little corn,
For weary man to trouble born!

For labour, food; for all their own:
Our right to trade from zone to zone,
To make all laws for us and ours,
And curb the will of evil powers.

———

Printed by A. Whitaker and Co., Iris Office.

Glossary and notes

Since the Chartists were active during the late 1830s and early 1840s we have included two items all closely connected with Unions. The first is a notice calling on Englishmen to refuse to pay taxes until the working class receive freedom. The second is the hymn composed by Ebenezer Elliott for the Chartists meeting at Sheffield in 1838 and lays stress on food, for at this time there was activity for the repeal of the Corn Laws.

RULES

UNANIMOUSLY AGREED TO BY THE MEMBERS OF THE

COAL MINERS' UNION,

IN MIDDLETON AND ITS VICINITY,

On the First of July, 1819.

First Rule.

IN order to enable the Widow, Relatives, or Executors of any legal Brother Member, to inter him in a Christian-like Manner, when it shall please God to take him hence, every surviving Brother in the Township of Middleton, shall pay *Two-pence* : and the Monies so raised shall be intrusted to one Man in each Pit, to be by him paid down at the Funeral to the Person entitled to receive the same. And every Member is requested to attend the Funeral, unless detained by work or sickness.

Second Rule.

WHEN any Member's Wife dies, the Widower shall have *One-penny* per Man paid to him, for one Wife only, to enable him to inter her decently: and should he be married to a second, and she should survive him, then she shall have the other *Penny* paid at his death. No member will be required to attend her Funeral.

Third Rule.

ALL Learners shall pay *One Penny* each at the death of any legal Member; and when a Learner dies, every legal Member and Learner shall pay *One Penny* each towards his Interment. Every Learner and all single Men are requested to attend the Funeral, unless prevented by Work or Sickness.

Fourth Rule.

SHOULD any Member be under the necessity of leaving the Business in Middleton and its Vicinity, and still continue to contribute to Funerals as above specified, an information thereof, which information shall be given by the Pitmates he last worked with, if required by him on his leaving; he shall be entitled to the Benefits as fully as if employed at one of the Pits in the District before-mentioned.

Fifth Rule.

IF any Member is found guilty of boasting of his Earnings, or of exposing any Rules of, or Benefits arising from, the Trade, to any Person not belonging thereto, or of boasting thereof to another Member in any Public-House, he shall forfeit and pay *Ten Shillings* for every Offence. And if any Member quarrels or fights with any of his Pitmates, or Brothers in the Trade, he shall pay *Two Shillings and Sixpence* for every Offence. The above Sums to be disposed of as his Pitmates may think proper: and any Member incurring any of the above Penalties, and refusing to pay after a demand thereof, he shall lose all claims to the benefits of these Rules.

EDWARD BAINES, PRINTER, LEEDS.

Private collection of P Burgoyne Johnson

Glossary and notes

Middleton colliery miners got round the combination Acts by making their union work like a friendly society. Members are forbidden to speak in public about the union rules or the benefits which they receive.

133 The Elsecar miners write to Earl Fitzwilliam, their employer, during their 1858 strike

My Lord

We the workmen employed at your Lordship's Colliery at Elsecar, humbly beg to call your Lordship's attention to our present distressed and some of us actually starving, condition. In doing so we wish to remind your Lordship of the promise made to us in 1844 when an Union was formed of the miners . . . and when your Lordship wrote a letter forbidding us to join that Union . . . and we were immediately to withdraw on pain of being discharged accompanied with a promise that we should be placed in as good or . . . better position than other workmen in any other Coal Establishment. We were obedient to your Lordship's commands . . . but in consequence of an Union being formed of the Masters to regulate the Price, Weight and Transit of Coal, our trade has declined at Elsecar until it has reached the present distressing state. The reason is clear . . . that the neighbouring Collieries do not act up to the regulations agreed . . . as your Lordship does . . .

Your Lordship's
Humble Servants

Sheffield City Libraries, Wentworth Woodhouse Muniment, T.29

Elsecar Nov. 5 1858

My Lord

As the Strike at the above Collieries unhappily does not terminate and as we are informed. [we] will receive no communication . . . in writing we submit the following item for your consideration.

We are willing to resume our Labour at the Prices we gave over at. But we are informed that we . . . [must] discontinue joining the Miners Friendly Society. We wish to inform you that the above Society is not such a thing of abhorence . . . as may have been represented to you as its rules only imply industry, humanity and Charitableness and to conduct ourselves with propriety both at our Labour and before the Public. We are devoted to Your Lordship . . . as we ever were Should Your Lordship desire an interview with us we have a deputation chosen to wait upon your call.

My Lord, we remain your Humble Servants

The Miners of Elsecar Collieries

Sheffield City Libraries, Wentworth Woodhouse Muniments T.29

Glossary and notes

The coal owners also formed associations to maintain prices and control wages. This meeting at Wakefield on 2 December 1836 shows you the type of business they transacted.

134 The meeting of
a coal owners'
association

AT A MEETING

OF THE UNDERMENTIONED COAL-OWNERS,

Held at the White-Hart Inn, Wakefield,

ON FRIDAY, THE 2nd DECEMBER, 1836:

PRESENT :—

Messrs. S. COOPER,
WAUD,
BRIGGS,
TWIBELL,
PICKARD, (for Sir J. L. Kaye,)
WESTMORELAND,
J. CHARLESWORTH,

Messrs. SMITHSON,
BIRAM, (for Earl Fitzwilliam,)
CASSON,
HOPWOOD,
CLARKE,
FIELD,
THOMAS WILSON.

MR. THOMAS WILSON IN THE CHAIR.

THE FOLLOWING RESOLUTIONS WERE AGREED TO:—

I.—It being reported that Messrs. THORP & Co., of Gawber Colliery, and Messrs. CLAYTON, of Kippax, do not comply with the late Act of Parliament, which directs Coals to be sold by Weight only,—

IT WAS RESOLVED UNANIMOUSLY,

That a remonstrance from this Meeting be sent to those Parties, requesting them to comply with the Act, by weighing their Coals, and informing them, that in case of their not doing so, an Information will be laid against them.

II.—That each Coal-Owner who neglects to attend the Half-yearly Meetings, shall pay a fine of Half-a-Guinea each time.

III.—That on the first of January next, an advance of Sixpence ℔ Ton take place on all Lime Coal.

IV.—That on the first of January next, an advance of Sixpence ℔ Ton on Riddled Slack, is desirable.

V.—That the next Meeting be held at the King's Head Inn, BARNSLEY, on the first Wednesday in June (6th), at Eleven o'Clock.

VI.—That the Resolutions of the Half-yearly Meetings be printed, and sent by the Chairman to all the Coal-Owners of the District.

THOMAS WILSON, *Chairman.*

135 A penny
reading

CHRIST CHURCH.

A PENNY READING

WILL (D.V.) BE GIVEN IN THE

SCHOOL-ROOM,
BURTON ROAD,

ON FRIDAY, DEC. 22,

TO BEGIN AT EIGHT O'CLOCK.

PROGRAMME.

HYMN	
SONG—"The child's first grief,"	THE SCHOOL CHILDREN
READING—"The abuse of Genius," from Pollock's "Course of Time,"	Rev. R. M. MASON
SONG—"In happy moments,"	Mr. FREARSON
RECITATION	Mr. JOB WOOD
SONG—"The fairy ring,"	THE SCHOOL CHILDREN
SOLO CONCERTINA	Mr. CRAXWELL
READING—"The Lancashire ballads,"	Mr. H. BEMROSE
GLEE—Awake Æolian lyre,"	THE CHOIR
READING—"How a printer was managed,"—2nd Part,...	Rev. C. M. BENSON
SONG—"The heart bowed down,"	Mr. CLARKE

GOD SAVE THE QUEEN.

ADMISSION ONE PENNY.

Working Men specially invited.

R. KEENE, PRINTER BY STEAM POWER, DERBY.

Derby Central Library

Glossary and notes

Penny readings were lectures (costing 1*d* entrance) arranged for working
men. They took place frequently about the middle of the nineteenth century.
This one seems to be more entertaining than educational!

BELPER TEMPERANCE SOCIETY

NEW YEAR'S TRACT.

"REAL PAIN IN THE MORNING."

"CHAM-PAGNE AT NIGHT."

Derby Central Library

Glossary and notes

Great efforts were made to encourage working-class men and women not to waste money on beer, gin and other drink. Many Temperance Societies were formed. This is the heading on a tract, or leaflet, printed for the Temperance Society in Belper in the 1830s. The rest of the tract consists of a long sermon on the evils of alcohol.

Education

137 Sheffield Mechanics' Library, 15 September 1832

The object of this Institution is to supply, at a *Cheap Rate* to different classes of the community, those advantages of *Instruction* in the various branches of *Science* and *Art*, which are of practical application to their diversified avocation and pursuits. This object is proposed to be attained—

1. By Systematic Courses of Lectures on Mechanics, Chemistry, and other branches of Natural or Moral Philosophy . . . but more especially those which are immediately applicable to or connected with the . . . Manufactures of this town.
2. By the purchase of Philosophical and Chemical Apparatus . . . necessary to the advancement of Scientific Knowledge.
3. By Instruction in Writing—Elements of English Grammar—Composition—higher branches of Mathematics—Drawing—and the principles of Mechanics Chemistry etc to be given in the evenings by competent Masters as soon as sufficient have joined the Institution. . . .

Sheffield City Libraries, 485M. Miscellaneous Papers

138 Regulations of Sheffield Mechanics' and Apprentices' Library, 27 December 1823

1. Apprentices and Youths may be admitted to the privilege of reading by a quarterly contribution of one shilling to be paid in advance; their parents, masters or other respectable persons shall guarantee them to be proper persons.
2. The apprentices are expected not to loiter unnecessarily in the library, and they are strictly enjoined not to lose any time in their way to and from the room, as any well founded complaint on this score from their employer will be followed by expulsion.
3. The Library books must not be lent from one young man to another.
4. The Committee shall prohibit the use of such books which for their great value or any other cause they think improper for young readers.

Sheffield City Libraries, Leader Collection 513

WELL BEGUN IS HALF DONE

Sheffield Central National School.

Scholar's Certificate.

The undersigned certify that *Charles Smith* aged *13* years at the date hereof, has attended the above-named School for *7½* years, and that *he* can now read *fluently* write a *good* hand, work sums as far as *Vulgar Fractions* and that *his* knowledge of

Holy Scripture is	*fair*	Grammar is	*good*
Church Catechism	*fair*	English History	*fair*
Geography	*fair*		

During the whole time that *he* has been in the above-named School, *his* conduct has been *very satisfactory, & quite correct in all respects.*

Signed this *28th* day of *July* 185*8*

Henry James Certified or Registered Teacher.

Name *S. Earnshaw*
Address *Sheffield*
Name *Thomas Sorby*
Address *Sheffield*
Name *Edward Hudson*
Address *Sheffield*

Managers of the School.

Parochial Clergyman.
H. M. Inspector of Schools.

Sheffield City Libraries, M.D. 192–M

Glossary and notes

Full time education to the age of thirteen was available at the national school and the grammar school. This scholar's certificate shows you the subjects taught and the standard attained in arithmetic.

Public Opinion
and Legislation

Introduction

The good and the bad sides of the factory system were discussed among people in general, and especially in Parliament. Many people wrote of the 'good old days' before factories had been heard of. Others thought that, as factories had obviously come to stay, the best thing to do was to improve conditions of life for those who had to work in them. Whether or not the law should allow children to work in mills was also an important question.

Child labour had been abused under the Domestic system but no one had noticed the long hours they worked at home nor the early age at which they were set to do some domestic task. They lived in crowded, ill-ventilated rooms amongst the tools of the domestic clothier's trade; it was not an ideal system.

When the factories were built the children were employed in large numbers and attention was drawn to the conditions under which children worked and people like Richard Oastler began to work for reform in factories.

'Reformers' As early as 1784 the Lancashire Justices of Peace had decided they would sign no more parish apprenticeship papers because children were employed on night work. Robert Owen gave evidence to a Parliamentary Commission on employment of children. Richard Oastler wrote letters to the papers and went around the West Riding speaking about 'white slavery'—that is the employment of children in factories under conditions no better than the Negro slaves in America. As a result of their work the first successful Factory Act was passed in 1833 followed by the Ten Hours Act in 1847.

No action was taken about employment of women and girls in mines until 1842. No survey of mines had been made and the outcry against child labour in mines did not develop until the factory reformers had won their case.

'Conservatives' The manufacturers feared that any reduction of hours would mean harm to the factory workers and would eliminate the profits made by the owner. Their views were expressed in a report to Parliament in 1834 in which they stated that to eliminate child labour would destroy the future of the textile industry. In the same way the coal owners like Lord Londonderry opposed reform in mines on the grounds that children were happy doing menial tasks underground and to eliminate their labour would destroy the profitability of the mines.

In the domestic system of manufacture which obtained in the West Riding of Yorkshire, when I was a boy, it was the custom for the children at that time, to mix learning their trades with other instruction and with amusement, and they learned their trades or their occupations, not by being put into places, to stop there from morning till night, but by having a little work to do, and then some time for instruction, and they were generally under the immediate care of their parents; the villages about Leeds and Huddersfield were occupied by respectable little clothiers, who could manufacture a piece of cloth or two in the week, or three, or four or five pieces, and always had their family at home: and they could at that time make a good profit by what they sold; there were filial affection and parental feeling, and not over-labour; but that race of manufacturers has been almost completely destroyed; there are scarcely any of the old-fashioned domestic manufacturers left, and the villages are composed of one or two, or in some cases of three or four, millowners, and the rest, poor creatures who are reduced and ground down to want, and in general are compelled to live upon the labour of their little ones.

140 The 'good old days'

Glossary and notes

Richard Oastler is giving evidence to a Parliamentary Committee in 1832. He was an estate agent in Yorkshire. Here he is comparing the small manufacturers of the West Riding domestic system about 1800 with the rich millowners of the 1830s. The growth of mechanization and the factory system in the woollen industry was about 20 or 30 years later than in the cotton industry.

When the lace machinery was brought to Tiverton in 1816, the ancient woollen manufacture was so wretchedly depressed, that the labouring population was little employed and worse paid. The town had become the residence of military and naval officers on half-pay since the peace of 1815, who no doubt chose it because of its mild climate and cheap provisions, perhaps also for the advantage of an ancient endowed school. The advent of such an addition to the population as that employed by this factory, gradually raised the prices of everything, to the annoyance of some; but the compensative result to the retail trade was very remarkable. An officer came there to reside, and remarked in the hearing of an old and experienced collector of King's taxes, that 'the coming thither of lace machinery had ruined Tiverton'. On which the other rejoined, 'I can shew by my books, that in 1816 there were not three shop-keepers in High street,' (the principal street), 'who could pay their taxes regularly, and that now (1826) there are not three that owe any.' Its old importance as a borough returned with the arrival of HEATHCOTE, and has remained ever since.

141 How a factory gave employment

W. Felkin, 'The History of the Machine-Wrought Hosiery and Lace Manufactures', 1867

Glossary and notes

Some districts benefited from factories being set up. This extract from Felkin's book on the hosiery industry points out the change in Tiverton, Devonshire, after Heathcote set up a lace factory there.

HEATHCOTE   the owner of a lace factory at Loughborough in Leicestershire which was attacked in 1816, and £10,000 worth of machinery was destroyed. Six of the Luddites were hanged and two transported for life. Heathcote swore never to set up in the Midlands again, and he immediately moved to Tiverton. His factory there employed about 1,200 people.

At the following Mills there are Apprentices

Mellor. Mr Oldknow. very clean

Any commendation of mine must fall short of
Mr Oldknow's very meritorious conduct towards the
Apprentices under his care, whose comfort in every
respect seems to be his study: they were all look
-ing very well and extremely clean.

Litton Mill. Mr Ellis Needham - Clean

I found the house, in which the Apprentices ~~lodge~~
board, & lodge, very clean: but two of them having
come to me, with a complaint of being worked too
hard, and of not having sufficient support, I thought
it right to examine some of the Apprentices upon
Oath as to the facts they complained of, and the
substance of their deposition is as follows: viz.
"That they go into the Mill about ten minutes
before six o'clock in the morning, and stay there
till from ten to fifteen minutes after nine in
the evening, excepting the time allowed for din-
-ner, which is from half, to three quarters of an
hour, that they have water-porridge for break-

fast and supper and generally oatcake and treacle or oatcake and poor broth for dinner; that they are instructed in writing and reading on Sundays." Mr. John Needham said that the Mill was useless, and the apprentices unemployed for a month in the winter in consequence of putting down a water wheel.

Cressbrook Mill. Mr. William Newton. Clean.
Upon enquiring of the Apprentices here, how they lived, I received for answer, "that they go into the Mill at six o'clock in the morning and come out again at eight o'clock in the evening, that they have an hour allowed for dinner, are very comfortable, and live well." Their diet consists of milk, or milk porridge for breakfast, and supper, and they have flesh meat every day at dinner. They looked well and appeared perfectly satisfied with their situation. The following new Appointment of visitors was made at this Sessions

145

[illegible] Report was delivered in at this Sessions

Leam 18th Apl 1811

Report of Cotton Mills and Factories inspected
from the last Midsummer Sessions to the present
date, by me _____ H H Middleton

Names of Mills. Masters & overlookers. Condition of the Mill

1 Dinting	}	Mr Thos Chadwick. Clean
2 Shipley	} near Glossop	John Shaw. {Directed to be whitewash'd & the upper room ventilated}
3 Bridge End		George Burgess.– Clean
4 Shipley Mill Glossop		Robert Shipley. Dirty
5 Whitfield	} near Glossop	Messrs J & W Winshaw. Very clean
6 Charlstown	}	Mr George Robinson. Clean
7 Hayfield		Aron Barnsley. Requires ventilation
8 Goddard	}	James Pottek. Do
9 Torr	} At New Mills	Danl Stafford – Do & white-washing
10 Groves	}	Charles Walker.. Do & – Do

At the above Mills no Apprentices were taken

Glossary and notes

The first Factory Act 1802 was called the Health and Morals of Apprentices Act. In it, the Justices of the Peace were given the job of inspecting cotton mills to see that the factory apprentices were not ill-treated. They also had to see that mills were clean and properly ventilated. Here are some pages from a J.P.'s notebook. (For Cressbrook Mill see also p. 76. For Litton Mill see also p. 78.) The story of Robert Blincoe is told in *A Textile Community in the Industrial Revolution* (see Further Reading p. 158).

DO.   short for ditto, meaning the same as the one before.

143 Yorkshire 'slavery'

SLAVERY IN YORKSHIRE.

TO THE EDITORS OF THE LEEDS MERCURY.

"It is the pride of Britain that a Slave cannot exist on her soil; "and if I read the genius of her constitution aright, I find that "Slavery is most abhorrent to it—that the air which Britons "breath is free—the ground on which the y tread is sacred to "liberty."—*Rev.* R. W HAMILTON's *Speech at the Meeting held in the Cloth-hall Yard, Sept. 22d, 1830.*

GENTLEMEN,—No heart responded with truer accents to the sounds of liberty which were heard in the Leeds Cloth-hall yard, on the 22d inst. than did mine, and from none could more sincere and earnest prayers arise to the throne of Heaven, that hereafter Slavery might only be known to Britain in the pages of her history. One shade alone obscured my pleasure, arising not from any difference in principle *to the whole Empire*. The pious and able champions of *Negro* liberty and *Colonial* rights should, if I mistake not, have gone farther than they did; or perhaps, to speak more correctly, before they had travelled so far as the West Indies, should, at least for a few moments, have sojourned in our own immediate neighbourhood, and have directed the attention of the meeting to scenes of misery, acts of oppression and victims of Slavery, even on the threshold of our homes!

Let truth speak out, appalling as the statements may appear. The fact is true. Thousands of our fellow-creatures and fellow-subjects, both male and female, the miserable inhabitants of a *Yorkshire town*; (Yorkshire now represented in Parliament by the giant of anti-slavery principles,) are this very moment existing in a state of Slavery *more horrid* than are the victims of that hellish system—"*Colonial Slavery*." These innocent creatures drawl out unpitied their short but miserable existence, in a place famed for its profession of religious zeal, whose inhabitants are ever foremost in *professing* " Temperance" and " Reformation," and are striving to outrun their neighbours in Missionary exertions, and would fain send the Bible to the farthest corner of the globe—aye in the very place where the anti-slavery fever rages most furiously, her *apparent charity*, is not more admired on earth, than her *real cruelty* is abhorred in heaven. The very streets which receive the droppings of an "Anti-Slavery Society" are every morning wet by the tears of innocent victims at the accursed shrine of avarice, who are *compelled* (not by the cart-whip of the negro slave-driver) but by the dread of the equally appalling thong or strap of the overlooker, to hasten, half-dressed, *but not half-fed*, to those magazines of British Infantile Slavery—*the Worsted Mills in the town and neighbourhood of Bradford!!!*

Would that I had Brougham's eloquence, that I might rouse the hearts of the nation, and make every Briton swear "These innocents shall be free!"

Thousands of little children, both male and female, *but principally female*, from SEVEN to fourteen years of age, are daily *compelled to labour* from six o'clock in the morning to seven in the evening, with only—Britons blush whilst you read it!—*with only thirty minutes allowed for eating and recreation!*—Poor infants! ye are indeed sacrificed at the shrine of avarice, *without even the solace of the negro slave;*—ye are no more than he is, *free agents*—

ye are compelled to work as long as the *necessity* of your needy parents may require, or the cold-blooded avarice of your worse than barbarian masters *may demand!* Ye live in the boasted land of freedom, and *feel* and mourn that *ye are Slaves*, and slaves without the only comfort which the Negro has. He knows it is his sordid mercenary master's INTEREST that he should *live*, be *strong* and *healthy*. Not so *with you*. Ye are doomed to labour from morn till night for one who cares not how soon your weak and tender frames are stretched to breaking! You are not mercifully valued at so much per head; this would assure you at least (even with the worst and most cruel masters), of the mercy shown to their own labouring beasts. No, no! your soft and delicate limbs are tired, and fagged, and jaded at only *so much per week*; and when your joints can act no longer, your emaciated frames are cast aside, the boards on which you lately toiled and wasted life away, are instantly supplied with other victims, who in this boasted land of liberty are HIRED—not sold—as Slaves, and daily forced to *hear* that they are free. Oh! Duncombe! Thou hatest Slavery—I know thou dost resolve that " Yorkshire children shall no more be slaves." And Morpeth! who justly gloriest in the Christian faith—Oh Morpeth listen to the cries and count the tears of these poor babes, and let St. Stephen's hear thee swear—" they shall no longer groan in Slavery!" And Bethell, too! who swears eternal hatred to the name of Slave, whene'er thy manly voice is heard in Britain's senate, assert the rights and liberty of Yorkshire Youths. And Brougham! Thou who art the chosen champion of liberty in every clime! Oh bend thy giant's mind, and listen to the sorrowing accents of these poor Yorkshire little ones, and note their tears; then let thy voice rehearse their woes, and touch the chord thou only holdest—the chord that sounds above the silvery notes in praise of heavenly liberty, and down descending at thy will, groans in the horrid caverns of the deep in unuttering sounds of misery accursed to hellish bondage; and as thou soundst these notes, let Yorkshire hear thee swear " Her *children* shall be free!" Yes, all ye four protectors of our rights, chosen by freemen to destroy oppression's rod,

" Vow one by one, vow altogether, vow
" With heart and voice, eternal enmity
" Against oppression by your brethren's hands;
" Till man nor woman under Britain's laws,
" Nor son nor daughter born within her empire,
" Shall buy, or sell, or HIRE, or BE a Slave!"

The nation is now most resolutely determined that Negroes shall be free. Let them, however, not forget that Briton's have common rights with Afric's sons.

The blacks may be fairly compared to beasts of burden, *kept for their master's use*. The whites to those *which others keep and let for hire!* If I have succeeded in calling the attention of your readers to the horrid and abominable system on which the worsted mills in and near Bradford are conducted, I have done some good. Why should not children working in them be protected by legislative enactments, as well as those who work in cotton mills? Christians should feel and act for those whom Christ so eminently loved and declared that " of such is the kingdom of heaven."

Your insertion of the above in the *Leeds Mercury*, at your earliest convenience, will oblige, Gentlemen,

Your most obedient servant,

RICHARD OASTLER.

Fixby-Hall, near Huddersfield, Sept. 29th, 1830.

British Museum, 'Leeds Mercury,' 16 October 1830

144 Black and white slavery

NEGRO SLAVERY.   ENGLISH LIBERTY.

University Library Glasgow

Glossary and notes

Richard Oastler (see p. 143) started a campaign in 1830 which was to lead to the passing of the first effective Factory Act in 1833. About this time, many people were demanding that Parliament should set free Negro slaves on British plantations in the West Indies. Notice how Oastler makes the point that the factory children are slaves in all but name and that in fact they are worse off than the West Indian slaves. Duncombe, Morpeth, Bethell and Brougham were the names of the M.P.s for Yorkshire at the time.

Robert Cruikshank, the artist, made the same point in a series of cartoons.

145 Robert Owen answers M.P.s' questions about reducing hours of work for children

Do you think that the regulations which are in force at New Lanark would apply to a large, populous manufacturing town, where the inhabitants are not utterly dependent upon a manufactory?

The same principles, I conceive, may be applied, under different modifications, to any situation, where there are few or many.

What employment could be found for the children of the poor, in those situations, till 10 years of age?

It does not appear to me that it is necessary for children to be employed under 10 years of age, in any regular work.

If you did not employ them in any regular work, what would you do with them?

Instruct them and give them exercise.

Would there not be a danger of their acquiring, by that time, vicious habits, for want of regular occupation?

My own experience leads me to say that I have found quite the reverse, that their habits have been good in proportion to the extent of their instruction.

Parliamentary Report on child labour in cotton mills

Glossary and notes

From 1802 onwards Parliament began to take an interest in the conditions of child workers in factories. One question was whether small children should be employed at all. In this extract, Robert Owen, the owner of the 'Model Factory' at New Lanark is answering questions put by a Committee of M.P.s in 1816.

146 The Strutts' view, given to Parliament in 1834

The reduction of time from twelve hours to ten, and the consequent reduction of wages, would have a most serious and lamentable effect on the working class, as well as bring a great injury to the master. Everything should be done to enable the working class to procure sufficient food and clothing, and the comforts of life, and then there is some chance of making some moral improvement, but it is very difficult to instruct and improve the hungry and the naked, and those who are degraded (against their own will too) into pauperism.

Report of Factory Commission, 1834

Glossary and notes

This is the opinion of the Strutts stated in 1834. By the 1833 Factory Act, the older children's work was set at a maximum of twelve hours per day. The Strutts were regarded as benevolent employers but here they are objecting to any further reduction in the hours of work.

147 An argument against change

Water-gilding was very pernicious to those employed in it, yet it was not under the operation of any legislative restriction. The plate glass business was allowed to be highly insalubrious. Children, however, were employed in it, though exposed to violent heats and draughts of air. Glass-cutting also was unhealthy. The work was carried on in damp places; people of tender age were employed in it, but yet, in none of these cases did the Legislature think it necessary to interfere. Was the weaving trade less unwholesome than the cotton? And were not children put to it at as early an age, and kept as long at work? The weaver was pent up in a long, close, confined cabin, and often obliged to work upon a damp floor. Working people were exposed to the vicissitudes of excessive heat and cold, to damps of every kind, and to every species of bodily infirmity in the coal and lead mines, and yet nobody ever called for such legislative enactments in the management of those concerns.

Select Committee on the state of children employed in Manufactories, 1816

Glossary and notes

Some Members of Parliament were against any changes. This is a report of what Lord Stanley said in a debate in 1818. The argument is that as there are evils in many industries it is therefore wrong to pick any one industry and try to improve it. By 'the weaving trade' he meant the woollen industry.

VICISSITUDES   alternations.

148 Opposition to a Bill

The spinners engaged in opposing this Bill disavow the abuses with which they have been charged. Anxious that the truth should appear, they, previously to the Session of 1816, invited such Members of the House of Commons as are connected with this county, to visit the several factories in this town and neighbourhood, that they might, from actual inspection, and comparison, form their own opinions, and be better prepared to appreciate the testimony which might be offered. In the present Session they have presented a Petition to the House of Commons, praying for the appointment of a Special Commission of their own body, for the purpose of examining, upon the spot, into the actual conditions of persons employed in factories, and of comparing it with that of persons employed in any of the various departments of the cotton trade and other manufactures.

Such an investigation would ascertain how far the evidence of facts coincides with assertions founded rather upon mere theoretical opinions, or upon partial and prejudiced views of the question.

If the Bill should pass into law, many hands under sixteen years of age will be inevitably turned out of employment, and, in all probability, thrown upon the parish. An influx from the country of persons above sixteen years of age, to supply their places, will necessarily follow.

The Bill of 1815 extended to all buildings, in all trades, in which twenty or more persons are employed under eighteen years of age. The present Bill is limited to buildings in which cotton yarn is made. But it would be the height of inconsistency in Parliament to legislate for one branch of manufacturing labour, and not embrace the whole; the injurious consequence of which, not only to the manufacturer, but as affecting the poor's rates, must be obvious.

House of Commons Debates on Factory Bill, 1818

Glossary and notes

Attempts to get Parliament to pass laws about the treatment of child workers, or about hours and conditions of work, always met with opposition. This extract is from a broadsheet published by cotton spinners in Manchester, to arouse opposition to Sir Robert Peel's Bill in 1818. The Bill proposed a twelve-hour maximum working day for all children under sixteen in cotton mills, and a minimum age of nine. It was passed in 1819.

THE TEN HOURS' BILL.

TO THE FACTORY OPERATIVES OF LANCASHIRE.

FELLOW WORKPEOPLE,

The present position of the Ten Hours' Bill now before the House of Commons demands your most serious attention. On your exertions, in a very great degree, depends the success or failure of our present struggle. The Central Committee, ever anxious to consult the factory workers in such times of difficulty, have deemed it their duty to call a Delegate Meeting from every town in Lancashire, to consider the best course now to be adopted, and to lay down certain rules to guide the delegates in their course of procedure in London. A statement of the accounts of the Committee will be laid before the meeting, and every other information which they possess.

The meeting will be held on Sunday, April 19th, 1846, at the OLD SWAN INN, *Pool Street, Market Street*, near the Post Office, Manchester.

It is particularly requested that each district will send at least one delegate, as the business to be brought before the meeting will be important.

Before the time of meeting Lord Ashley and Mr. Fielden will be communicated with on the subject, and their advice taken as to what is the best course to be adopted, which will, of course, be laid before the meeting.

The Chair to be taken at Ten o'clock in the Morning precisely.

JOSEPH MULLINEAUX, SEC.

N.B.—All communications in future to be addressed to the Secretary, Old Swan Inn, Pool Street, Market Street, Manchester.

Manchester Public Libraries

Glossary and notes

In 1833, after great discussion in Parliament and outside, the first effective Factory Act was passed. To its supporters this was only the beginning; not the final victory. Another Act was passed in 1844; and yet another, called the Ten Hours Act, in 1847. This is a leaflet advertising a meeting in Manchester to support the Bill in 1846.

A Return of the Apprentices in the Cotton Mills within the Parish of *Glossop* in the Hundred of *High Peak*

Names of Parishes.	Names of Mills.	Names of Proprietors of Mills.	Names of Apprentices in each Mill during the last ten years, ending Christmas, 1840.	Where from if out of the County.	When Bound.	Between whom Indentures made.	When they left, and where went to.	Whether Parish Apprentice or not.	Remarks.
Glossop	Milton Mill	John Clayton & Co.	Mary Ryan		7 May 1835		7 May 1842 — Myple	Not	
Do	Do	Do	Ann Swift		Do		22 Oct 1841 — Dead		
Do	Do	Do	Ellen Corrigan		Do		7 Nov 1841 Myple		
Do	Do	Do	Hugh Leigham		June Do		2 Aug 1842 Dead		
Do	Do	Do	Ann Lynch	Southampton	Sept 1 1835		20 Sept 1842 Dead		
Do	Do	Do	Mary Ryan		1 June 1835		whore 1842 Mare		
Do	Do	Do	Lydia Pugh		22 Aug 1835		22 May 1842 London		
Do	Do	Do	Ann Jones		15 Nov 1835		absconded		
Do	Do	Do	Ann Templin		20 Nov 1835		20 Nov 1842 Murra		
Do	Do	Do	Jane Rowley		1 Dec 1835		1 Dec 1842 Do		
Do	Do	Do	Ann Moore		Aug 1835		Nov 1842 Myple		
Do	Do	Do	Sophia Howard		12 Jan 1836		Nov 1842 Do		
Do	Do	Do	Mary Simpson		11 Feby 1836		11 Feby 1842 Absham		
Do	Do	Do	Mary Galvin		20 March 1836		20 March 1842 Dead		
Do	Do	Do	Mary Ryan		21 April 1836		21 April 1842 Married		
Do	Do	Do	Ann McGowen		25 May 1836		25 May 1842 Do		
Do	Do	Do	Mary Cowley		25 May 1836		25 May 1842 Dead		
Do	Do	Do	Jane Marsh		7 June 1836		7 June 1842 Murra		
Do	Do	Do	Sarah Estall		8 July 1836		8 July 1842 London		
Do	Do	Do	Catharine Swift		27 June 1837		27 June 1842 London		
Do	Do	Do	Charlotte Malony		12 July 1837		12 July 1842 Dead		
Do	Do	Do	Charlotte Dunbar		9 Aug 1837		9 Aug 1842 Myple		
Do	Do	Do	Elizabeth Hill		17 July 1837		17 July 1842 London		
Do	Do	Do	Mary Lynch		8 Nov 1837		8 Nov 1842 Myple		
Do	Do	Do	Margaret Cooper		23 Nov 1837		23 Nov 1842 Do		
Do	Do	Do	Mary Hough		14 Feby 1838		14 Feby 1842 Married		
Do	Do	Do	Ann Carroll		15 Feby 1838		15 Feby 1838 Dead		

Derbyshire County Record Office, Apprentices, 1840

Glossary and notes

Parliament had to be very careful in the wording of factory laws. When mill owners were prevented from taking apprentices from parish workhouses, some employers hired them from military and naval orphanages instead. This document illustrates this. Notice where the children are from, and that none of them are parish apprentices.

... the trapper's employment is neither cheerless nor dull nor stupefying; nor is he, nor can be, kept in solitude and darkness all the time he is in the pit. The working trap-doors are all placed in the principal passages, leading from the bottom of the pit to the various works, so that an interval of seldom more than five minutes but generally much less passes without some person passing through his door, and having a word with the trapper. Neither is the trapper deprived of light by any means general, as the stationary lights on the trolly and tramways are frequently placed near the trapper seat.

The trapper is generally cheerful and contented, and to be found like other children of his age, occupied in making models of windmills, waggons etc. and frequently in drawing figures with chalk on his door, modelling figures of men and animals in clay etc. . . .

Hansard Debates, House of Lords 24 June 1842

151 A coal owner reacts to the 1842 Report on the Mines

Glossary and notes

The reports on conditions in textile factories led to the setting up of a Commission in 1840 to enquire into conditions in mines and manufactures. The first report appeared in May 1842 and dealt with the employment of children, young persons and women in mines, iron works and steel works. One of the commissioners, Dr Southwood Smith, believed that M.P.s were too busy to read long reports so he included illustrations of the working conditions they found in the report. These successfully aroused public opinion. The Marquess of Londonderry, a very influential Durham coal owner opposed any legislation on the employment of children and was furious when he saw the pictures in the report.

152 A report on ventilation in the mines, 1849

Sheffield City Libraries

Ventilation shafts are those with the exhaust openings.

What is the ordinary ventilation in the Yorkshire Collieries?

By a furnace at the bottom of the upcast shaft.

You examined Darley Main Pit after the accident?

Yes I was down the pits after the accident both at Ardsley Main and Darley Main.

You are aware that it is the practice to make full use of water to create a downward current in the downcast shaft?

We are using that method in a new pit at Elsecar . . . there is a very considerable quantity of carburetted hydrogen in the main . . . as to render a furnace dangerous; the only method we have of ventilating the pit is by a small stream of water turning down the engine pit . . . it creates a considerable draught.

I have applied a stream of water falling . . . 78 feet . . . at about 10 gallons a minute . . . upon the circumference of a wheel four feet in diameter; when the winds were in a certain direction it acted well and produced a great draught, but in other situations of the wind it did not.

. . . but with a fan on that principle, fixed . . . in an upcast shaft, a little above the surface of the ground, and worked by a sufficient steam power . . . I still think in many cases where it might be dangerous to use a furnace in a pit, a very great draught might be obtained by that mechanical means. . . .

Parliamentary Papers, Ben Biram's evidence before the Select Committee
On Safety in Mines, 2 July 1849

LINES UPON THE
CATASTROPHE AT BARNSLEY,
CAUSED BY THE EXPLOSION AT THE
OAKS COLLIERY,
BY WHICH,
UPWARDS OF 300 PERSONS
LOST THEIR LIVES, Dec. 12, 1866.

COMPOSED AND SPOKEN BY
E. I. HART,
Author of "THE CONSTELLATIONS," lines upon the
"LATE LORD PALMERSTON," &c.

Hark! What noise was that—a smother'd roar
That seems to come from the earth's very inmost core!
Tis past—'tis gone—and yet it seems to have cast
A spell that make men stare and look aghast.

Alas, too well that fatal sound is known,
And quick succeeds the human shriek and groan,
As rushing from their homes in frantic dread,
Mother—Sister—Wife—the roads now tread.

The quiet country round no longer seems
Buried in repose—for hurrying streams
Of people throng the whole country side,
Hoping against hope—trying their fears to hide.

At last the fatal shaft is gain'd—but Oh!
To mark those agonizing looks of woe—
To think that 'neath the very ground we tread,
Our dear one's lie—scorch'd—dying—perhaps dead.

While we stand idly here, without the power
To even sooth them in their dying hour;
Crush'd—broken hearted—gazing in silent gloom
At the blacken'd "shaft" that leads to that mighty tomb.

But down that fatal "shaft" more men must go;
Who'll volunteer to brave the peril? Who'll go below?
'Tis almost certain death! Will any try
To end suspense—to know the worst, or die?

Ah! ah! won't they—you scarce the question ask,
E're thrice the number wanted's ready for the task;
However poor the "collier," uncouth his look and way,
When help is needed, he never yet said nay.

For those who face the cannon's mouth, the pen
Is often raised!—equal are not these men?
Yet rare we think it worth our while to write,
For those who toil in everlasting night.

The "cage" once more is fix'd on high, and fill'd
To secure the dying—to recover the kill'd;
Brave hearts are there, and science also lends
Her chosen sons, to further still their ends.

Hark! surely not again! Great Heaven! No, no!
That dreadful roaring sound! That scream of woe!
'Tis so—all gone—the men that went to save,
All buried in one vast and burning grave.

Let those who blame the "Collier," when he asks
For a fair day's wage for his dangerous, hazardous tasks;
Look upon desolate scenes like these, and say—
Who, more than "The Miner" deserves his pay.

J. WHITE, 104, WESTBAR, AND PARADISE-ST., SHEFFIELD.

Illustrated London News 22 December 1866.

154 The Coal Mines Regulation Act, 1842

An Act to prohibit the employment of women and girls in mines and collieries, to regulate the employment of boys, and to make other provisions relating to persons working therein.

That from and after the passing of this Act it shall not be lawful for any owner of any mine or colliery whatsoever to employ any female person within any mine or colliery, or permit any female person to work or be therein for the purpose of working therein, other than such as were at or before the passing of this act employed within such mine or colliery, and that from and after three calendar months from the passing of this act it shall not be lawful for any owner of any mine or colliery to employ any female person who at the passing of this act shall be under the age of eighteen years within any mine or colliery. . . .

That from and after the first day of March, one thousand eight hundred and forty-three, it shall not be lawful for any owner of any mine or colliery to employ any male person under the age of ten years . . . other than such as at the passing of this act shall have attained the age of nine years, and were at or before the passing of this act employed within such mine or colliery.

That it shall be lawful for one of Her Majesty's principal Secretaries of State, if and when he shall think fit, to appoint any proper person or persons to visit and inspect any mine or colliery; and it shall be lawful for every person so authorised to enter and examine such mine or colliery . . . at all times and seasons, by day or by night, and to make inquiry touching any matter within the provisions of this act. . . .

No provision of the Act to affect employment on the surface.

And whereas the practice of paying wages to workmen at public houses is found to be highly injurious to the best interests of the working classes; be it therefore enacted, that from and after the expiration of three months from the passing of this act no proprietor or worker of any mine or colliery or other person, shall pay or cause to be paid any wages . . . at or within any tavern, public house, beer shop or other house of entertainment.

Wages so paid can be recovered as if no payment made.

Statutes of the Realm, 1842

Glossary and notes

This Act was passed as a result of the Report of 1842.

A Note on the Songs

The ballad seller was a feature of English life from Tudor times until within living memory. With his sheaves of penny broadsides, some in his hat, he would trudge the markets and fairs, streets and lanes, in country and town. To attract custom, he would sing out his ballads. Sometimes a tune was specified at the head of a sheet, sometimes it was evident from the title or metre. Otherwise, the ballad singer would fit a tune from the store in his memory. He might make small alterations to his texts, so that they fitted the tune, or flowed more smoothly off the tongue.

Many of the songs included here were, or originated as, broadside ballads. In presenting them, the ballad singer's practice with tunes and texts has been followed, so as to ensure that the songs will be sung. The small changes have in no way altered the character of the pieces.

All the tunes used are traditional. The texts, including the ballad by Joseph Mather of Sheffield, are in the traditional idiom which, contrary to received opinion, was often used in urban, as well as rural, folk song. This is not the place for a detailed analysis of traditional style, but it should be remembered that these songs were sung in the streets, the alehouses and the factories because they expressed the fears, the hardships, the bitterness and the exuberance of people struggling to come to terms with their environment. The tunes are often fine but the words should always be clear. The melody is printed as it fits the first verse; small rhythmic variations must be made by the singer to avoid making nonsense of the other verses.

The sources of the songs and recorded performances (though not necessarily of the same version) are listed in the sources. The following books and records are also recommended.

Books
Ewan MacColl and Peggy Seeger, *The singing island*, Mills Music, 1960.
M. Dawnay, *The iron man*, Galliard, 1974.
Roy Palmer, *Songs of the Midlands*, E.P. Publishing, Wakefield, 1972.
A. L. Lloyd, *Folksong in England*, Lawrence and Wishart, 1967.
J. Raven, *Songs of a changing world*, Ginn, 1973.

Records

Topic Records Ltd,
  27 Nassington Road,
  London NW3 2TX.
  Along the coaly Tyne, 12T189.
  The iron muse, 12T86.
  Owdham edge, 12T204.
  Tommy Armstrong of Tyneside,
  12T122.
  The wide Midlands, 12T210.
  A Lancashire mon, 12TS236.
  Transpennine, 12TS215.
  The bitter and the sweet, 12TS217.
  Oldham's burning sands, 12TS206.

Best o' t' bunch, 12TS237.
Jack of all trades, 12TS159.
Argo Records,
  Decca,
  9 Albert Embankment,
  London SE1.
  The angry muse, ZDA83.
  The big hewer, RG538.
Leader Sound Ltd,
  209 Rochdale Road,
  Greetland, Halifax,
  Yorkshire HX4 8JE.
  Jack Elliott of Birtley, LEA 4001.

Further Reading

Other manuscript and documentary records of the Textile Industry are to be found at Leeds City Archives; Manchester Central Library (Local History Section); Lancashire Record Office, Preston; Nottingham Record Office; The British Records Association, Charterhouse Square, London have details of all records in the hands of local record offices throughout the country.

James Watt and Steam Power, Cape (Jackdaw 13).

E. G. Power: *A Textile Community in the Industrial Revolution*, Longman (Then and There).

K. McKechnie: *A Border Woollen Town in the Industrial Revolution*, Longman (Then and There).

S. Ellacot: *Spinning and Weaving*, Methuen (Outlines of History).

G. Ghorbals: *Huddersfield Woollen & Worsted Industry*, Tolson Memorial Museum publications, Huddersfield.

Stella Davies: *Living Through the Industrial Revolution*, Routledge 1966.

I. Temen: *This England 1714–1960*, Macmillan, pp. 30–33: 109–129.

J. Addy: *A Coal and Iron Community in the Industrial Revolution*, Longman (Then and There).

S. Ellacot: *Forge and Foundry*, Methuen (Outlines of History).

M. Tomalin: *Coal Mines and Miners*, Methuen 1960.

W. K. V. Gail: *Iron and Steel*, Longman (Industrial Archaeology).

A. Raistrick: *A Dynasty of Ironfounders*, Darbys and Coalbrookdale 1970.

J. D. Marshall: *Furness and the Industrial Revolution*, Barrow Library.

G. C. Helen: *Railways*, Blackwell.

E. Garnett: *Master Engineers*, Hodder & Stoughton.

L. T. C. Rolt: *Brunel*, Penguin 1970.

M. O. Greenwood: *Railway Revolution 1825–1845*, Longman (Then and There).

J. A. Williamson: *George & Robert Stephenson*, A. & C. Black.

A. Robertson: *The Trade Unions*, Hamish Hamilton.

J. J. Bowles: *Dramatic Decisions*, Macmillan.

Peter Searby: *The Chartists*, Longman (Then and There).

N. Wymer: *Social Reformers*.

The Early Trade Unions, Cape (Jackdaw 35).

M. Hutchinson: *Education in Britain*, Hamish Hamilton.

P. F. Speed: *Learning and Teaching in Victorian Times*, Longman (Then and There).

Charles Dickens: *Nicholas Nickleby*.